DISCARDED

Econometric Dimensions of Energy Demand and Supply

Econometric Dimensions of Energy Demand and Supply

Edited by
A. Bradley Askin
John Kraft

Lexington Books
D. C. Heath and Company
Lexington, Massachusetts
Toronto

Library of Congress Cataloging in Publication Data

Main entry under title:

Econometric dimensions of energy demand and supply.

   Includes index.
   1. Energy policy—United States—Addresses, essays, lectures.
2. Power resources—United States—Addresses, essays, lectures.
I. Askin, A. Bradley. II. Kraft, John.
HD9502.U52E27   333.7   75-21872
ISBN 0-669-00032-9

Copyright © 1976 by D.C. Heath and Company

All rights reserved. No part of this publication may be reproduced or transmitted in any form or by any means, electronic or mechanical, including photocopy, recording, or any information storage or retrieval system, without permission in writing from the publisher.

Published simultaneously in Canada

Printed in the United States of America

International Standard Book Number: 0-669-00032-9

Library of Congress Catalog Card Number: 75-21872

To V.C.T.
his stories are better than these stories

To M.J.K.
her dreams are too

Contents

	List of Figures	ix
	List of Tables	xi
	Preface	xv
Chapter 1	The Growing Importance of Energy Policy and Analysis *A. Bradley Askin*	1
Chapter 2	A National Energy Demand Simulation Model *John Kraft, Arthur Kraft, and Eugene Reiser*	9
Chapter 3	The Capital Stock Adjustment Process and the Demand for Gasoline: A Market-Share Approach *Derriel Cato, Mark Rodekohr, and James Sweeney*	29
Chapter 4	Demand for Fossil Fuels by Electric Utilities *Scott E. Atkinson and Robert Halvorsen*	53
Chapter 5	An Application of Spatial Equilibrium Analysis to Electrical Energy Allocation *Noel D. Uri*	65
Chapter 6	Short Term Forecasts of Energy Supply and Demand *Christopher Alt, Anthony Bopp, and George Lady*	81
Chapter 7	The Macroeconometric Implications of Alternative Energy Scenarios *A. Bradley Askin*	91
Chapter 8	Alternative Energy Policies' Impact on Industry Price Behavior *Paul H. Earl and Steven G. Phillips*	111
	About the Contributors	125
	About the Editors	127

List of Figures

3–1	Partitioned Automobile Class	32
3–2	Flow Chart of Gasoline Demand Model	42
3–3	Small Car Sales—Selected Scenarios	47
3–4	Medium Car Sales—Selected Scenarios	48
3–5	Large Car Sales—Selected Scenarios	49
3–6	(a) New Car Sales-Weighted MPG—Selected Scenarios; (b) Projected Gasoline Demand—Selected Scenarios	50
7–1	Flow Chart of PIES and Macroeconomic Analyses	93
7–2	Quantity Impacts Associated with the Same Price Changes Induced by Demand versus Supply Shifts	97
8–1	BAU11 versus BAU7 Energy Indexes	114
8–2	$7 Scenarios	115
8–3	$11 Scenarios	116

List of Tables

1–1	U.S. Petroleum Imports Since 1950	4
2–1	Physical Unit Conversion Factors	11
2–2	Energy Demands in the Industrial Sector	12
2–3	Energy Demands in the Household—Commercial Sector	13
2–4	Estimated Statistics for Total Demand in Industrial and HHC Sectors	15
2–5	Estimated Statistics for Electricity/Fossil Fuel Share: 1955–1972	19
2–6	Estimated Statistics for Fossil Fuel Shares in Industrial Sector	19
2–7	Estimated Statistics for Fossil Fuel Shares in Household—Commercial Sector	20
2–8	Error measures for 1955 to 1972 for Fuels: Industrial Sector	21
2–9	Error Measures for 1955 to 1972 for Fuels: Household-Commercial Sector	21
2–10	Short Run Own- and Cross-Price Elasticities: Industrial Sector	22
2–11	Short Run Own- and Cross-Price Elasticities: Household-Commercial Sector	23
2–12	Long Run Own- and Cross-Price Elasticities: Industrial Sector	24
2–13	Long Run Own- and Cross-Price Elasticities: Household-Commercial Sector	25
3–1	Parameter Estimates of Hedonic Equation over Time	33
3–2	Estimated Demand Equations for Small, Medium, and Large Cars	37
3–3	Market Share Elasticities	43
3–4	Technology Elasticities	44
3–5	Income Elasticities	45

3-6	Gasoline Elasticities	46
4-1	Estimated Demand Equations	59
4-2	Estimated Elasticities of Demand and Substitution	60
4-3	Predicted and Actual Fuel Consumption, 1974	61
5-1	Equilibrium Demand for Electrical Energy by Sector and Region, 1973	73
5-2	Equilibrium Flows of Electrical Energy Generated in 1973	74
5-3	Equilibrium Generation by Plant Type and Region, 1973	75
5-4	Equilibrium Demand Price by Region, 1973	76
5-5	Quasi Rent of a Particular Plant Type, 1973	77
5-6	Quasi Rent on Transmission Restriction, 1973	78
6-1	Petroleum Product Price Elasticities	84
6-2	Dynamically Specified Economic Activity Elasticities	85
6-3	Statically Specified Economic Activity Elasticities	85
6-4	Petroleum Product Detail Demand: Comparison of FEA Forecast with BOM Actual	89
7-1	Percent Differences in 1985 Price Levels Between Other Scenarios and the $11 BAU Scenario	102
7-2	Differences in 1985 Real GNP Levels Measured in Billions of 1958 Dollars Between Other Scenarios and the $11 BAU Scenario	103
7-3	Differences in 1985 Real Investment Levels Measured in Billions of 1958 Dollars Between Other Scenarios and the $11 BAU Scenario	105
7-4	Percentage Point Differences in 1985 Unemployment Rates and Capacity Utilization Rates for Manufacturing Between Other Scenarios and the $11 BAU Scenario	106
7-5	Differences in 1985 Real Personal Consumption Expenditure Levels Measured in Billions of 1958 Dollars Between Other Scenarios and the $11 BAU Scenario	107

8–1	Peak Difference Between Business as Usual and Combined Conservation and Accelerated Development ($7)	118
8–2	Peak Difference Between Business as Usual and Combined Conservation and Accelerated Development ($11)	120

Preface

All the essays presented in the following pages were prepared for this book; none has appeared in print elsewhere. We want to thank all the contributors for their efforts to undertake this project and make it a worthwhile one. Although the pressures of deadlines and other commitments have prevented us from including everything we originally intended to, the eight chapters contained in this volume provide considerable insight into the current state of economic research on energy.

With one exception, all the chapters were written by people associated with the Federal Energy Administration (FEA). Much of the work reported in this volume could not have been carried on outside FEA. We wish not only to acknowledge the financial support and services supplied by FEA, but also to express our appreciation to colleagues and superiors for creating and maintaining an environment conducive to this type of publication effort. At the same time, however, we wish to stress that all views and opinions expressed in this book are those of the individual chapter contributors. They should not be attributed to the authors of other chapters; they do not represent the official, or unofficial, position of FEA.

Several people assisted above and beyond the call of duty in putting this book together. Renee Barnow reviewed all chapters for content and style and prepared the material appearing at the front and back of the book. Jean Rosar typed most of the manuscript, some of it more than once. Debbie McGee and Laurie Hardman also typed portions of the manuscript. Michael McCarroll of Lexington Books graciously extended our deadline several times when our good intentions conflicted with the hectic pace at FEA. As in past collaborations, each of us cheerfully assigns the blame for all errors to the other.

1

The Growing Importance of Energy Policy and Analysis

A. Bradley Askin

The Rise of OPEC

The agreement by Iran, Iraq, Kuwait, Saudi Arabia, and Venezuela at a conference among them held September 10–14, 1960, in Baghdad, Iraq to form an Organization of Petroleum Exporting Countries (OPEC) attracted scant notice in the United States. For instance, the *New York Times* did not report either the agreement or the conference until almost two weeks later, September 25, 1960, when it ran a four paragraph news story on page 3 and presented a by-lined analysis covering parts of three columns in the Sunday financial section [2, 7]. Various oil producing nations had banded together for years, dating back at least to the formation of the Arab League in 1944, without achieving any apparent success in promoting their interests. Everyone knew that cartels inevitably broke down from competition among their members.[a]

During most of the 1960s, OPEC experienced limited success in achieving its goals. It was able to freeze posted prices, thereby preventing further reductions in them; increase taxation, which captured a larger share of profits for producing country governments; and perhaps marginally speed up participation and relinquishment. All these accomplishments helped its member states. Yet OPEC was unable to meet either of its two main objectives: raising prices and controlling production. Supply grew more rapidly than demand, and new production areas gained at the expense of old ones, as prices measured in real terms declined. Evaluating OPEC's performance up to 1969, Edith Penrose concluded that OPEC had exerted a "relative lack of influence on the structural changes in the oil industry over the last ten years" [10, p. 158]. Writing two years later, Fuad Rouhani, the first secretary general of OPEC (1961–1964), lamented "ten years of failure" to do more than arrest the downward trend in prices [11, p.4].

Toward the end of the 1960s, OPEC gradually began to play a more powerful role in world oil affairs. In 1968 it won acceptance of royalty expensing from the major oil companies in its battle for larger tax payments. That same year it issued a declaratory statement announcing the consolidation of common policies that went beyond previous expressions

---

The first section of this chapter is based on [1], [6], [8], [9], [10], and [11].

[a]For a review of this position and an informative discussion of cartels, see [3].

1

of objectives and explicitly called for participation by producing countries in the operation of oil fields. In 1970 a shift from excess supply to excess demand conditions in the world market for crude oil enabled OPEC to negotiate the Tehran agreements of February 1971.[b] These agreements raised the price of crude oil measured in real terms after many years of decline. Thereafter OPEC raised the price of crude oil measured in real terms each year through 1973.

Finally, during the two weeks following an October 17, 1973, meeting of the Arab members of OPEC (OAPEC) that was called to discuss the outbreak of war between Egypt and Israel, the main Arab oil producing nations imposed production cutbacks and an embargo on all petroleum shipments to the United States and the Netherlands that lasted until March 17, 1974.

The U.S. Response

Table 1–1 summarizes the course of U.S. petroleum imports since 1950. Up to 1970 the average price at which crude oil was imported remained fairly stable in nominal terms and declined in real terms. After 1970 it rose in both nominal and real terms, particularly after the Arab embargo. The volume of both crude oil and total petroleum imports rose steadily over the entire period, except for the last two years which have been marked by recession and embargo induced conservation efforts. Expenditures on petroleum exports rose consistently throughout the period, reflecting the steady growth in the volume of imports and the recent surge in the average price of imports.

The Arab oil embargo forced the United States to recognize immediately two ominous patterns evident in Table 1 – 1 that had previously been accorded only passing attention: the growing reliance on insecure foreign supplies of petroleum stemming from growing demand and declining domestic production, and the increasing transfer of purchasing power abroad to pay for petroleum imports.[c] On December 4, 1973, slightly more than a month after the start of the Arab oil embargo, President Nixon signed Executive Order 11748, creating a Federal Energy Office (FEO) which later became the Federal Energy Administration (FEA). The Presi-

---

[b]Fuad credits the rapid growth in demand with causing the shift [11, p. 4]. McKie also mentions production cutbacks in Libya and the disappearance of excess capacity in the United States [6, pp. 51–52].

[c]In 1970 a cabinet task force appointed by the president warned that OPEC "might form an effective cartel that would charge us 'a monopoly price,' " before concluding, "but that seems unlikely" [12, pp. 12, 35].

dent gave the new agency instructions to undertake planning and analysis for "Project Independence," among other duties.[d]

After a year of effort involving thousands of manhours, extensive computer simulations of complex economic models, and probably a cost of several million dollars, in November 1974 the Federal Energy Administration released a voluminous *Project Independence Report* examining the implications of several alternative U.S. energy strategies [5]. Based on an econometric model of energy demand and a fixed-point programming model of energy supply solved together, this report presented equilibrium forecasts of prices, consumption, domestic production, and imports for different energy sources under a variety of assumptions about government policy, technology, and the world price of crude oil as set by OPEC.[e]

About This Book

This book presents a set of econometric, policy oriented studies on energy to provide a glimpse of current research in the energy economics field. Some of the chapters report on studies directly connected to FEA's Project Independence, while others bear either no relationship or only a peripheral relationship to it. We have attempted to place the chapters in a logical order, but each chapter was written independently by its authors.

In Chapter 2, John Kraft, Arthur Kraft, and Eugene Reiser describe a national energy demand model. The model treats, in price and income sensitive fashion, both the major and minor fuels consumed by the household, commercial, and industrial sectors of the economy. A key feature of the model is the handling of competition among fuels in a multiple logit framework that ensures fuel shares consistent with total energy consumption.

Chapter 3, by Derriel Cato, Mark Rodekohr, and James L. Sweeney, introduces a vintage capital stock model of gasoline demand based on a submodel of automobile demand by classification categories. This represents an advance over previous studies, which have used simple flow adjustment models to implicitly represent the capital stock of automobiles or have ignored the capital stock of automobiles completely. The study

---

[d]The Federal Energy Administration Act of 1974 transformed the FEO into the FEA as of June 27, 1974.

[e]The second major report reflecting additions and modifications of the various models and extensive simulation studies was published in early 1976 [4]. Planning for a third report is now in progress.

Table 1-1
U.S. Petroleum Imports Since 1950

(1) Year	(2) Customs Average Unit Value of Crude Oil Imports (per Barrel)	(3) Real Customs Average Unit Value of Crude Oil Imports (per Barrel)	(4) Annual Volume of Crude Oil Imports (Millions of Barrels)	(5) Volume of Crude Oil Imports as Percentage of Domestic Crude Production (%)	(6) Annual Value of Crude Oil Imports (Millions of Dollars)
1950	$ 2.12	$2.65	174	8.8	$ 369
1955	2.23	2.45	294	11.8	655
1960	2.23	2.16	401	15.6	895
1961	2.27	2.17	412	15.7	935
1962	2.24	2.12	451	16.9	1,012
1963	2.25	2.10	455	16.5	1,025
1964	2.24	2.06	483	17.3	1,080
1965	2.23	2.01	502	17.6	1,120
1966	2.25	1.97	496	16.4	1,115
1967	2.27	1.93	469	14.6	1,064
1968	2.25	1.83	527	15.8	1,184
1969	2.28	1.78	569	16.9	1,298
1970	2.36	1.74	535	15.2	1,260
1971	2.51	1.78	671	19.4	1,687
1972	2.64	1.81	897	26.0	2,369
1973	3.27	2.12	1,098	38.6	4,241
1974	11.19	6.58	1,362	42.5	15,253
1975	$11.57	$6.25	1,581	51.8	$18,290

(1) Year	(7) Customs Average Unit Value of Total Petroleum Imports (per Barrel)	(8) Real Customs Average Unit Value of Total Petroleum Imports (per Barrel)	(9) Annual Volume of Total Petroleum Imports (per Barrel)	(10) Volume of Total Petroleum Imports as Percentage of Domestic Petroleum Consumption (%)	(11) Annual Volume of Total Petroleum Imports (Millions of Dollars)
1950	$ 1.88	2.35	309	13.0	$ 580
1955	2.18	2.40	470	15.2	1,026
1960	2.25	2.18	687	19.4	1,544
1961	2.28	2.18	717	20.0	1,637
1962	2.25	2.13	785	21.0	1,765
1963	2.29	2.13	780	20.2	1,782
1964	2.37	2.18	827	20.9	1,963
1965	2.39	2.16	901	21.8	2,153
1966	2.35	2.06	940	21.7	2,209
1967	2.17	1.85	1,072	23.9	2,329
1968	2.24	1.84	1,113	22.7	2,498
1969	2.32	1.81	1,237	23.9	2,876
1970	2.22	1.64	1,243	23.2	2,759
1971	2.32	1.64	1,447	26.1	3,360
1972	2.59	1.77	1,695	28.3	4,383
1973	2.76	1.79	3,017	47.8	8,339
1974	11.03	6.48	2,218	36.5	24,449
1975	$15.60	$8.42	2,185	36.7	$ 34,077

Source: Department of the Interior, Bureau of Mines, unpublished data; Department of Commerce, Bureau of Economic Analysis. National Income Accounts data.

Note: Columns 3 and 8 are computed by dividing columns 2 and 7, respectively, by the implicit GNP deflator.

shows that categorical classification of automobile demand is crucial for determining long run gasoline demand.

In Chapter 4, Scott E. Atkinson and Robert Halvorsen employ translog functions derived from duality theory to estimate the own and cross elasticities of demand and substitution for alternative fuels in electricity generation. The study utilizes Zellner's method for estimating seemingly unrelated regressions with pooled time series and cross-section data. The authors find that changes in relative fuel prices induce substantial substitution among fuels.

Chapter 5, by Noel D. Uri, examines the advantages and disadvantages of switching from the present system to a regionally integrated system of electrical generation and distribution. Uri constructs a linear programming model with a quasi-welfare objective function, uses translog regression equations with pooled time series and cross-section data to estimate parameters for the objective function and constraints, and then applies the linear programming model. He concludes that operating electric utilities on a national basis would yield net benefits to society.

In Chapter 6, Christopher B. Alt, Anthony E. Bopp, and George M. Lady report on a short term petroleum forecasting model developed at FEA. The model forecasts aggregate petroleum consumption for eight different fuels in a dynamic framework that recognizes the influences of their prices, weather conditions, and the level of macroeconomic activity.

Chapter 7, by A. Bradley Askin, explores the problems involved in assessing the macroeconomic impacts associated with alternative energy strategies. Askin describes three separate methodologies, discusses their limitations, and then presents three sets of forecasts for the economy in 1985 based on eight energy scenarios considered in *Project Independence Report*.

In Chapter 8, Paul H. Earl and Steven G. Phillips employ a disaggregated price model to examine the relative price impacts alternative energy policies have at the individual product level. The model is built around a detailed energy input matrix covering approximately 100 product and material prices, including, for example, 10 types of steel. Earl and Phillips apply the model to the same scenarios Askin considers in Chapter 7.

References

[1] Adelman, M.A. "Politics, Economics, and World Oil." *American Economic Review* 64, no. 2 (May 1974): 58–67.

[2] Carmical, J.H. "World Oil Cartel May Take Shape." *New York Times,* September 25, 1960, sec. III, p. 1.

[3] Danielson, Albert L. "Cartel Rivalry and the World Price of Oil." *Southern Economic Journal* 42, no. 3 (January 1976): 407–415.
[4] Federal Energy Administration. *National Energy Outlook*. Washington, D.C.: U.S. Government Printing Office, 1976.
[5] ———. *Project Independence Report*. Washington, D.C.: U.S. Government Printing Office, 1974.
[6] McKie, James W. "The Political Economy of World Petroleum." *American Economic Review* 64, no. 2 (May 1974): 51–57.
[7] "Mideast Oil Lands Seek Price Stability." *New York Times*, September 25, 1960, p. 3.
[8] Mikdashi, Zuhayr R. *The Community of Oil Exporting Countries*. Ithaca, N.Y.: Cornell University Press, 1971.
[9] Parra, Francisco R. "OPEC: Present and Future Role." In Zuhayr M. Mikdashi, Sherril Cleland, and Ian Seymour, eds., *Continuity and Change in the World Oil Industry*. Beirut, Lebanon: The Middle East Research and Publishing Center, 1970. Pp. 135–147.
[10] Penrose, Edith. "OPEC and the Changing Structure of the International Petroleum Industry." In Zuhayr M. Mikdashi, Sherril Cleland, and Ian Seymour, eds., *Continuity and Change in the World Oil Industry*. Beirut, Lebanon: The Middle East Research and Publishing Center, 1970. Pp. 149–158.
[11] Rouhani, Fuad. *A History of O.P.E.C.* New York: Praeger Publishers, 1971.
[12] U.S. Cabinet Task Force on Oil Import Control. *The Oil Import Question*. A Report on the Relationship of Oil Imports to the National Security. Washington, D.C.: U.S. Government Printing Office, 1970.

2

A National Energy Demand Simulation Model

John Kraft, Arthur Kraft, and Eugene Reiser

Introduction

In this chapter we present and discuss an energy demand simulation model. The fuels modeled are the major and minor fuels used in the household-commercial (HHC) sector and the industrial (IND) sector. We use an econometric model to estimate the demands for fuel and power in these two sectors. The model can provide insights into the effects of higher fuel prices on the consumption of energy as well as the efficiency of fuel choice decisions between electricity and fossil fuels.

The model can also be used to predict selected fuel prices and quantities demanded by the household-commercial sector and industrial sectors.[a] Inputs to the energy demand model include assumptions about economic and demographic behavior. If used for forecasting purposes, the model would require assumptions about prices of crude oil and the other fossil fuels. The model is structured around the U.S. energy accounts. The data generated by the model are classified by fuel users and by fuel source with definitions consistent with those used by the Bureau of Mines.

The structure of the model and the specific variables incorporated vary between sectors, based upon structural differences between sectors. Although we discuss each sector individually, several characteristics are common to the modeling of each sector.

Unlike many other studies that consider the demand for a single fuel, we consider the total consumption of energy and competition among all fuels consumed.[b] The model we present allows for complete fuel substitution and computes the total demand for electricity and fossil fuels: coal, natural gas, kerosene, distillate fuel, liquefied petroleum gas, still gas, and petroleum coke.

Since the demand model is to be used for policy analysis, particular stress has been placed upon incorporating the variables that seem most

---

[a]This chapter focuses on the household-commercial and the industrial sector. However, two other chapters tend to focus on the transportation sector and the electric sector, and thereby complete the entire range of demands by fuel by sector.

[b]In particular, many researchers have considered the demand for a single fuel without considering the fuel substitution possibilities with respect to other fuels. For example, see Griffin [3], MacAvoy and Noll [8], and Kennedy [5]—only a few of the many studies that treat separately the demand for a single fuel (coal, natural gas, or petroleum).

susceptible to economic influence. Whenever feasible, the influences of prices of a given fuel and prices of its substitutes have been examined. Fuel prices, levels of industrial activity in various sectors, and the level of per capita GNP are incorporated whenever empirically justified. Provisions for incorporating other factors, such as changes in insulation standards and solar heat, can be built into the model.

We propose to analyze the patterns of fuel choice within the HHC sector and the IND sector by estimating a multiple logit model of fuel choice experience as explanatory valuables.[c] The advantage of this approach is that it allows us to consider a range of fuel choice experiences that satisfies total energy consumption. By constructing a model of fuel choice experience one can analyze energy policy decisions based on higher fuel costs.

The chapter is developed in three sections: the first section discusses the data base; the second, the model and simulation results; and the third, the conclusions and extensions of the model.

The Data Base

The data collected are annual time series on fuel consumption in the HHC and IND sectors of the United States from 1950 through 1972. The price and quantity data are recorded in common physical units: cents per Mcf, dollars per barrel, dollars per short ton, and cents per kilowatt-hour. However, to allow for complete substitution, all quantities and prices are converted to units in terms of heat content (Btu).

In an attempt to arrive at a complete equilibrium, we have converted all fuel quantities into Btu's and all prices into dollars per Btu using the conversion factors in Table 2–1. This approach allows comparison of prices and quantities in terms of equivalent heating units.[d] The approach is realistic in that large price differentials could not be maintained in the long run for fuels with equivalent heating potential. It is particularly relevant when one considers energy used for fuel and power purposes. On this basis, coal used for metallurgical purposes is excluded from the coal totals. Likewise, petroleum and natural gas products used as raw materials are also excluded from the consumption totals. All quantities are recorded in thousand trillion Btu's.

Before conversion to a Btu price, the prices were defined as follows: The electricity price was the marginal cost of electricity in cents per

---

[c]For a discussion of the theory of the multiple logit model, see Theil [12] and McFadden [9]. For empirical applications of this model, see Kraft and Kraft [6], *Project Independence* [2], and Schmidt and Strauss [11].

[d]The concept of "Btu equilibrium" is elaborated by Hausman [4].

Table 2–1
Physical Unit Conversion Factors

Approximate Heat Content of Various Energy Sources	
Petroleum	
Crude oil	5.800 million Btu/bbl
Refined products, average	5.508 million Btu/bbl
Gasoline	5.248 million Btu/bbl
Jet fuel, average	5.604 million Btu/bbl
Naphtha-type	5.355 million Btu/bbl
Kerosene-type	5.670 million Btu/bbl
Distillate fuel oil	5.825 million Btu/bbl
Residual fuel oil	6.287 million Btu/bbl
Natural gas liquids	3.99 million Btu/bbl
Natural gas	
Wet	1101 Btu/ft^3
Dry	1031 Btu/ft^3
Coal	
Bituminous and lignite	
Production	24.05 million Btu/short ton
Consumption	23.75 million Btu/short ton
Anthracite	25.40 million Btu/short ton
Hydroelectric power	10,379 Btu/kWh
Nuclear power	10,660 Btu/kWh
Electricity consumption	3,412 Btu/wKh

Source: *Monthly Energy Review* (Washington, D. C.: Federal Energy Administration, March 1976), p. 89.

kilowatt-hour computed from the Federal Power Commission's typical electric bills by customer classes. The natural gas price is the average price in cents per Mcf. All the petroleum products are average prices in dollars per barrel, and coal is bituminous or anthracite coal in dollars per short ton.[e] All prices reflect transactions for quantities actually received by the user. Natural gas was adjusted for pipeline transmission, and field use and electricity were adjusted for transmission loss. Distillate prices include taxes and dealer markups.

The Model and Simulation

The model developed is concerned with the determination of demands for fuel and power in the aggregate and their associated fuel substitution

---
[e]Consistent prices where available for all fuels except kerosene, still gas, liquefied petroleum gas, and petroleum coke. Because the definitions for the quantity series for these fuels have changed several times between 1955 and 1972, and because they are all light fuels, we decided to use a single price for each of these lighter fuels. For an explanation of this approach, see *Project Independence* [2].

possibilities. On the demand side, the bulk of the past empirical work has tended to focus on the demand for a particular fuel in terms of such variables as price, income, and population. Here we consider an entire range of fuels.

Industrial Sector

The basic procedure for predicting demands in the industrial sector is similar to that used in the household and commercial sector: A total energy demand equation is solved, and this total demand is then partitioned into shares.

Total demand for energy in the industrial sector is a function of a composite energy price and a measurement of industrial activity. The composite price is a weighted sum of energy prices in the industrial sector with weights corresponding to the energy shares in the industrial sector. The elasticity of total energy demand with respect to the price index is -0.097 in the short run and -0.119 in the long run. The measure of industrial activity is referred to as potential demand. The elasticity of energy output with respect to potential demand is 0.517 in the short run and 0.634 in the long run.

Once total energy demand is calculated, the shares of this demand satisfied by different products are calculated in a three-stage process. First the total demand is partitioned into demand for electricity and demand for fossil fuels (see Table 2–2). The share ratio depends upon the ratio of electricity price to the fossil fuel price. The elasticity of the share ratio with respect to the price ratio is -1.755 in both the short run and the long run. The shares in the ratio also depend upon the potential demand for fossil fuels with this elasticity equal to 1.914.

Fossil fuel in turn is partitioned into various products—natural gas,

Table 2–2
Energy Demands in the Industrial Sector

Total Energy Demand	
Electricity	*Fossil Fuels*
	Natural gas
	Bituminous coal
	Residual fuel
	Distillate fuel
	Liquefied gas
	Still gas
	Kerosene
	Petroleum coke

bituminous coal, residual fuel, distillate fuel, liquefied gases, still gas, kerosene, and petroleum coke.

Household-Commercial Sector

The model first predicts total energy consumed in the HHC sector as a function of the composite price of all fuels consumed in the HHC sector, the stock of housing, and real disposable income. The composite fuel price is a weighted sum of the fuel-specific energy prices where the weights correspond to the lagged shares of the total energy consumed in the previous years. The elasticity of total energy demanded in the HHC sector is -0.283 with respect to price, 0.857 with respect to the housing stock, and 0.525 with respect to disposable income. This equation is not dynamically specified and the long and short run elasticities are identical.

Once total energy demand in the HHC sector is calculated, the market shares of the various products are calculated by a one-stage procedure. Demand is partitioned into the fuel market shares with the ratio of shares depending upon the relative prices of the two products. The demand for all fuels is partitioned among the various products: electricity, natural gas, distillate fuel, residual fuel, kerosene, liquefied gases, and anthracite coal.

The share equations are constructed to assure that at both stages the sums of shares equal unity. This is accomplished by specifying equations that relate ratios of shares to price ratios. The multinomial extension of a logit function is used in these estimating equations. Actual shares are constructed from the share ratios plus the identity that the sum of shares must equal unity. This cascaded share approach is illustrated schematically in Table 2–3.

In predicting the total demand for energy in the household and commercial sector, we consider the stock of housing (*KHUS*) to be exogenous. This exogenously specified factor reflects the percentage difference

Table 2–3
Energy Demands in the Household-Commercial Sector

TOTAL ENERGY DEMAND
Electricity
Natural gas
Residual fuel
Distillate fuel
Kerosene
Still gas
Anthracite

in heating requirements between future additions to the housing stock and previous additions. As such, this provides a mechanism to incorporate conservation strategies aimed at influencing home insulation. Consumption is viewed as being composed of two steps, and a rise in the price of any fuel will bring forth two responses. First, the individual may try to substitute the relatively less expensive energy sources for the more expensive source. Second, the total demand for all energy resources may be reduced since the consumer may adjust the demand for the more expensive fuel by adjusting the utilization rate of the appliance or process using that fuel. Thus price adjustments produce fuel switching, but they also produce stock adjustments that influence the total demands for all energy sources.[f] Our efforts attempt to produce a model of the aggregate demands for fuel and power in the HHC sector and IND sector.[g]

Some attempts are made to incorporate adjustment dynamics into the model by using distributed lag formulations. The basic idea is that in response to changing conditions, economic agents will not move instantly to their new long run equilibrium consumption patterns but will gradually adjust from their original consumption patterns toward their new equilibria. This phenomenon can be partially captured by assuming that the current year's consumption is a function of the preceding year's consumption and the long run equilibrium level of consumption. However, it should be noted that even the use of such distributed lag equations generally is not sufficient to capture the dynamics of a rapid change from one state of the economy to another. The important point is that the model does not incorporate enough dynamic structure to allow precise approximations of the dynamics of rapid adjustment.

The model developed determines the total demands for energy in the HHC sector and the IND sector, and the fuel substitution possibilities within each of these sectors. While it would be desirable to separate the HHC sector into two separate sectors—residential and commercial—the data constraints eliminated this separation as a feasible option.

The overall model of energy consumption behavior in the HHC sector and the IND sector consists of two parts. The first part determines the total demands for fuel and power in the HHC sector and the IND sector. The second part of each model consists of a set of fuel-share equations estimated using multinomial logit functions. The basic sets of equations for each model are considered in the next section.

---

[f]The mechanism used in this research is not a complete stock adjustment model. For a better discussion of stock adjustment models, see the transportation sector model in Chapter 3 of this volume.

[g]The work for the industrial sector model draws on previously unpublished work by Kraft and Kraft [7].

Total Demand

Industrial Sector. The total demand for fuel in the industrial sector is estimated in double logarithmic form as a function of price, total potential demand, and a lagged value of total demand. *TOTFL* is the total energy consumed in the industrial sector and is the sum of both electricity and fossil fuels. *TOTPR* is a weighted average price of the prices of all fuels consumed in the industrial sector. Each price is weighted by the share of each fuel lagged one year. The remaining explanatory variables are *TOTFL* lagged one year and the potential demand for total fuel, *TOTPD*. The potential demand for total fuel is constructed from the potential demand for electricity and fossil fuels used in the industrial production. The lagged value of total fuel is used to give the model a dynamic adjustment mechanism. The potential demand provides a stock adjustment between actual and potential demand. It will later be seen that changes in potential demand reflect changes in economic activity within the industrial sector.

The form of the total demand equation is:

$$\ln(TOTFL) = \alpha_1 + \alpha_2 \ln(TOTPR) + \alpha_3 \ln(TOTFL(-1)) + \alpha_4 \ln(TOTPD). \quad (2.1)$$

In the equation, α_2 represents the short run price elasticity and should be negative while α_1, α_3, and α_4 are expected to be positive. The estimated values for Eq. (2.1) appear in Table 2–4.

Potential demands are computed for electricity (*ELCPD*) and fossil fuels (*FOSPD*). The sum of *ELCPD* and *FOSPD* is *TOTPD*, which is used

Table 2–4
Estimated Statistics for Total Demand in Industrial and HHC Sectors

Dependent Variable	Constant	ln(*TOTPR*)	ln(*TOTFL*(−1))	ln(*TOTPD*)
ln(*IND*)	9.523	−0.097	0.184	0.517
	(7.60)	(−1.26)	(1.61)	(8.70)

$\bar{R}^2 = 0.983$; D.W. = 1.419; S.E.E. = 0.166

	Constant	ln(*TOTPR*)	ln(*TOTYD*)	ln(*KHUS*)
ln(*HHC*)	2.78	−0.283	0.525	0.857
	(2.51)	(−1.90)	(2.41)	(1.48)

$\bar{R}^2 = 0.983$; D.W. = 1.791; S.E.E. = 0.0.44

Note: Numbers in parentheses are *t*-statistics.

in Eq. (2.1) to reflect the total potential demand for energy by the industrial sector. The potential demand for fuel, i, is defined as:

$$PD_i = \gamma_i(FRB), \qquad (2.2)$$

where PD_i is potential demand for fuel; γ_i is the ratio of fuel i to output originating in manufacturing; and FRB is the Federal Reserve Board index of industrial production.

The values of the γ_i's are computed as ratios of electricity and fossil fuels consumed to gross product originating in manufacturing from 1955 through 1972. The energy output ratio (γ_i) times the index of manufacturing output provides an approximation for potential demand. The idea is that as output increases, the demand for energy will increase based on increased activity in manufacturing and historical energy output ratios. For our model the potential demands are computed for two fuels: electricity ($ELCPD$) and fossil fuel ($FOSPD$).

Household-Commercial Sector. The total demand for fuel in the household-commercial sector is estimated in a manner similar to total industrial demand. The total demand is estimated in double logarithmic form as a function of price, the capital stock of housing, and real disposable income in 1958 dollars. Again $TOTFL$ is the total energy consumed in the HHC sector and is the sum of electricity and fossil fuels. $TOTPR$ is weighted average price of the fuels consumed in the HHC sector where each fuel is weighted by the lagged fuel shares. $TOTYD$ and $KHUS$ are real disposable income and the capital stock of housing. The income variable approximates the effect of income on the HHC demand for energy, while the stock of housing provides a structural input into the demand for energy. As the stock of housing increases, the demand for energy in the household sector increases. Likewise, if future units in the stock are more efficient than past units, the stock can be adjusted to reflect this improvement in equivalent units.

The form of the total demand equation for the HHC sector is:

$$\ln(TOTFL) = \alpha_1 + \alpha_2 \ln(TOTPR) \\ + \alpha_3 \ln(TOTYD) + \alpha_4 \ln(KHUS). \qquad (2.3)$$

In this equation, α_2 represents the short run elasticity of demand for fuel in the HHC sector with respect to aggregate fuel, while α_3 is the short run elasticity of demand with respect to income. The elasticity of demand with respect to the stock of housing is α_4. One would expect α_2 to be negative and α_3 and α_4 to be positive. The estimated coefficients for (2.3) appear in Table 2–4.

Fuel Shares

The basic procedure for determining demand in the industrial sector and the household-commercial sector is based on a logit-sharing scheme. Total energy demand in the IND and HHC sectors is determined by Eq. (2.1), (2.2), and (2.3), and then total demand is partitioned into fuel shares.

Total demand for energy in the industrial sector is a function of a weighted average of energy prices in dollars per Btu and some measure of industrial activity. Once total energy demand is calculated, the shares of the demand satisfied by the different energy products are calculated in a three-stage process. First, total demand is partitioned into demand for electricity and the demand for other fuels (fossil fuels). Fossil fuels are then partitioned into various products: natural gas, bituminous coal, residual fuel, distillate fuel, liquefied petroleum gases, still gas, kerosene, and petroleum coke (see Table 2–2). In the HHC sector we assume there is no structural difference in choosing between electricity and fossil fuels, but we partition total demand into electricity, natural gas, residual fuel, distillate fuel, kerosene, liquefied gas, and anthracite coal (see Table 2–3).

We now focus on a procedure for estimating the market shares for each energy source. In the past, considerable empirical work has been done using a linear model with the observed market share entered as the dependent variable. This approach is deficient for two reasons: (1) the expected value of the right-hand explanatory variables could be greater than one or less than zero; and (2) the disturbance term could suffer from heteroskedasticity.[h] Theil has corrected for this problem by developing the multinomial logit model that allows for the estimation of continuous left-hand variables confined to the zero to one range.[i]

Industrial Sector. We apply the multinomial logit model to the estimation of fuel market shares based on relative fuel prices, other choice characteristics, and lagged values of fuel shares. Each market share is computed as the total Btu's of fuel *i* relative to the total Btu's consumed. The fuel prices are measured in terms of dollars per Btu. The fuel characteristics are the potential demands for electricity (*ELCPD*) and the potential demands for fossil fuels (*FOSPD*).

First, the fuel share splits between electricity and fossil fuels are estimated, then the shares within fossil fuels are estimated. In the industrial sector there exists some question whether there is any substitution

---

[h]See Kraft and Kraft [6], Nerlove and Press [10], and Schmidt and Strauss [11] for further discussion of this point.

[i]For an evaluation of alternative techniques, see Kraft and Kraft [6] and Theil [12].

between electricity and fossil fuels: Fossil fuels are used basically for process heating, while electricity is used in special processes. The model, however, does allow for substitution between electricity and fossil fuels. The choice decision is treated as a separate hierarchy in that in the first stage the split is determined between electricity and fossil fuels and then splits are determined within fossil fuels.

The logit regression for the electricity fossil fuel decision is:

$$\ln(SELC/SFOS)_t = \beta_1 + \beta_2 \ln(PELC/PFOS)_t + \beta_3 \ln(ELCPD/FOSPD)_t \qquad (2.4)$$

where β_2 is expected to be negative and β_3 positive. The shares of electricity and fossil fuels are $SELC$ and $SFOS$, respectively. $PELC$ is the price of electricity and $PFOS$ is weighted average price of the fossil fuel prices. The share ratios are determined by the relative prices and the potential demands for these fuels. The summary statistics for Eq. (2.4) appear in Table 2–5.[j]

Within fossil fuels a series of multiple logit models are estimated for the fuel shares. For the years 1955 to 1972 we estimated functions of the form:

$$\begin{aligned}
\ln(SNG/SBIT)_t &= \beta_{11} + \beta_{12} \ln(PNG/PBIT)_t + \beta_{13} \ln(SNG/SBIT)_{t-1} \\
\ln(SRF/SBIT)_t &= \beta_{21} + \beta_{22} \ln(PRF/PBIT)_t + \beta_{23} \ln(SRF/SBIT)_{t-1} \\
\ln(SDF/SBIT)_t &= \beta_{31} + \beta_{32} \ln(PDF/PBIT)_t + \beta_{33} \ln(SDF/SBIT)_{t-1} \\
\ln(SSG/SBIT)_t &= \beta_{41} + \beta_{42} \ln(PSG/PBIT)_t + \beta_{43} \ln(SSG/SBIT)_{t-1} \quad (2.5) \\
\ln(SK/SBIT)_t &= \beta_{51} + \beta_{52} \ln(PK/PBIT)_t + \beta_{53} \ln(SK/SBIT)_{t-1} \\
\ln(SLG/SBIT)_t &= \beta_{61} + \beta_{62} \ln(PLG/PBIT)_t + \beta_{63} \ln(SLG/SBIT)_{t-1} \\
\ln(SPC/SBIT)_t &= \beta_{71} + \beta_{72} \ln(PPC/PBIT)_t + \beta_{73} \ln(SPC/SBIT)_{t-1}
\end{aligned}$$

where SNG, $SBIT$, SRF, SDF, SSG, SK, SLG, and SPC are, respectively, shares of natural gas, bituminous coal, residual fuel, distillate fuel, still gas, kerosene, liquefied gas, and petroleum coke. The first explanatory variable is the relative price ratio. From these equations we can derive other comparisons. For example, we know that

$$\ln(SNG/SDF)_t = \ln(SNG/SBIT)_t - \ln(SDF/SBIT)_t,$$

which yields:

---

[j] For estimation of the logit regression, a maximum likelihood or a weighted least squares approach may be used. For a discussion of these approaches see McFadden [9], Schmidt and Strauss [11], and Theil [12]. However, in our instances the data represented variations of national totals over time rather than cross-sectional observations in time, and thus we made no adjustment for heteroskedasticity. See Hausman [4] and Kraft and Kraft [6].

Table 2-5
Estimated Statistics for Electricity/Fossil Fuel Share: 1955–1972

	Constant	ln(PELC/PFOS)	ln(ELCPD/FOSPD)
ln[SELC/SFOS]	1.224	−1.755	1.914
	(2.58)	(−4.16)	(0.86)

$\bar{R}^2 = 0.842$; D.W. = 1.845; S.E.E. = .05556

Note: Numbers in parentheses are t-statistics.

$$\ln(SNG/SDF)_t = (\beta_{11} - \beta_{31}) + (\beta_{12} - \beta_{32}) \ln(PNG/PDF)_t \\ + (\beta_{13} - \beta_{33}) \ln(SNG/SDF)_{t-1}. \quad (2.6)$$

The summary statistics for the interval from 1955 to 1972 appear in Table 2-6.

A brief check of the results indicates that the logit regressions have the expected signs. The relative prices have negative coefficients—which imply, for example, that as the price of natural gas increases relative to the price of bituminous coal, the share of natural gas would decrease relative to the share of bituminous coal.

Household-Commercial Sector. In the HHC sector we determine the elasticity and fossil fuel demands directly from total demand without the intermediate sharing between electricity and fossil fuels. Unlike the in-

Table 2-6
Estimated Statistics for Fossil Fuel Shares in Industrial Sector

	$\hat{\beta}_{i1}$	$\hat{\beta}_{i2}$	$\hat{\beta}_{i3}$	$\bar{R}^2$	D.W.	S.E.E.
$\ln(SNG/SBIT)_t$	0.125 (1.80)	−0.117 (−1.13)	0.978 (15.72)	0.949	1.45	0.0751
$\ln(SRF/SBIT)_t$	0.103 (0.31)	−0.240 (−1.72)	0.978 (4.83)	0.635	1.64	0.0770
$\ln(SDF/SBIT)_t$	−0.123 (−0.29)	−0.520 (−1.03)	0.713 (2.33)	0.749	2.04	0.108
$\ln(SSG/SBIT)_t$	−0.032 (−0.19)	−0.224 (−2.15)	0.828 (6.17)	0.907	1.63	0.0577
$\ln(SK/SBIT)_t$	−1.232 (−2.12)	−0.055 (−0.34)	0.650 (4.20)	0.545	1.62	0.137
$\ln(SLG/SBIT)_t$	−2.03 (−2.51)	−1.005 (−2.79)	0.229 (0.95)	0.569	1.90	0.237
$\ln(SPC/SBIT)_t$	−0.232 (−0.82)	−0.149 (−0.59)	0.843 (6.12)	0.912	1.82	0.193

Note: Numbers in parentheses are t-statistics.

dustrial sector the choice decision is not one of electricity versus fossil fuels; instead, the hierarchy is a choice between electricity and each of the individual fossil fuels.

The fuel shares are estimated directly out of the total HHC sector demand by using a series of multiple logit models normalized with respect to electricity. Over the 1955 to 1972 time interval we estimated functions of the form

$$\ln(SNG/SELC)_t = \beta_{11} + \beta_{12} \ln(PNG/PELC)_t + \beta_{13} \ln(SNG/SELC)_{t-1}$$
$$\ln(SRF/SELC)_t = \beta_{21} + \beta_{22} \ln(PRF/PELC)_t + \beta_{23} \ln(SRF/SELC)_{t-1}$$
$$\ln(SDF/SELC)_t = \beta_{31} + \beta_{32} \ln(PDF/PELC)_t + \beta_{33} \ln(SDF/SELC)_{t-1} \quad (2.7)$$
$$\ln(SLG/SELC)_t = \beta_{41} + \beta_{42} \ln(PLG/PELC)_t + \beta_{43} \ln(SLG/SELC)_{t-1}$$
$$\ln(SBIT/SELC)_t = \beta_{51} + \beta_{52} \ln(PBIT/PELC)_t + \beta_{53} \ln(SBIT/SELC)_{t-1}$$
$$\ln(SK/SELC)_t = \beta_{61} + \beta_{62} \ln(PK/PELC)_t + \beta_{63} \ln(SK/SELC)_{t-1}$$

when the shares and the prices are defined identical to (2.7), except in this instance they apply to the HHC sector and not to the industrial sector. The estimated coefficients of Eq. 2.6 for the interval from 1955 to 1972 for the HHC sector appear in Table 2–7.

Simulations

To test the performance of the model of energy demand in the IND sector and the HHC sector, we combined Eqs. (2.1) through (2.5) into a complete model and solved it simultaneously. We simulated the model over

Table 2–7
Estimated Statistics for Fossil Fuel Shares in Household-Commercial Sector

	$\hat{\beta}_{i1}$	$\hat{\beta}_{i2}$	$\hat{\beta}_{i3}$	$\bar{R}^2$	D.W.	S.E.E.
$\ln(SNG/SELC)_t$	−0.335 (−4.10)	−0.243 (−2.80)	0.995 (16.87)	0.978	2.93	0.0219
$\ln(SRF/SELC)_t$	−0.521 (−1.08)	−0.390 (−1.91)	0.878 (1.53)	0.791	1.71	0.0868
$\ln(SDF/SELC)_t$	−0.260 (−0.72)	−0.122 (−0.53)	1.015 (17.67)	0.970	2.60	0.0555
$\ln(SLG/SELC)_t$	−0.411 (−0.86)	−0.158 (−0.76)	0.896 (5.89)	0.769	1.72	0.0542
$\ln(SBIT/SELC)_t$	2.43 (2.34)	−0.480 (−1.86)	0.841 (1.40)	0.989	1.92	0.0939
$\ln(SK/SELC)_t$	−0.937 (−1.19)	−0.488 (−1.11)	0.966 (15.58)	0.969	2.27	0.112

Note: Numbers in parentheses are *t*-statistics.

Table 2-8
Error Measures for 1955 to 1972 for Fuels: Industrial Sector
(in thousand trillion Btu's)

	M	MAE	MAE % M
Bituminous coal	4791.06	189.28	3.95
Natural gas	7123.02	262.81	3.69
Residual fuel	1215.03	120.82	9.94
Distillate fuel	403.41	36.41	9.03
Kerosene	126.91	18.38	14.48
Still gas	815.26	31.26	3.83
Petroleum coke	223.95	24.73	11.04
Liquefied petroleum gas	84.34	12.37	14.67
Electricity	1868.25	11.02	5.94

Note: The error measures are calculated according to the following formulae, where A_t denotes actual value, P_t the value predicted by the simulation, and T the number of observations contained in the simulation interval.

$$M = \frac{1}{T} \sum_{t=1}^{T} A_t$$

$$MAE = \frac{1}{T} \sum_{t=1}^{T} |A_t - P_t|$$

$$M \% MAE = M/MAE.$$

the 1955 to 1972 period. The mean of the actual series (M), the mean absolute error (MAE), and the mean absolute error as a percentage of the actual mean (MAE % M) are reported in Tables 2-8 and 2-9.[k]

Industrial Sector. While some of the MAEs are more than the series means, all the errors for the six largest energy sources are less than 10 percent. In fact, three fuels (natural gas, electricity, and bituminous coal) have errors less than 6 percent. When it is remembered that the errors are

---

[k]For a further interpretation of MAE and M % MAE, see Fair [1].

Table 2-9
Error Measures for 1955 to 1972 for Fuels—Household-Commercial Sector
(in thousand trillion Btu's)

	M	MAE	MAE % M
Natural gas	5375.5	207.60	3.86
Residual fuel	904.7	61.04	6.75
Distillate fuel	2729.5	158.30	5.79
Liquefied gas	516.2	32.82	6.35
Anthracite coal	647.8	58.96	9.10
Kerosene	438.5	33.99	7.75
Electricity	1943.4	77.04	3.96

Table 2–10
Short Run Own- and Cross-Price Elasticities: Industrial Sector

					Prices				
Quantities	PELC	PBIT	PRF	PDF	PNG	PK	PSG	PLG	PPC
Electricity	−1.662	0.305	0.103	0.083	0.659	0.250	0.250	0.250	0.250
Bituminous coal	0.058	−0.421	0.056	0.256	0.114	0.022	0.022	0.022	0.022
Residual fuel	0.058	0.509	−0.087	0.256	0.114	0.022	0.022	0.022	0.022
Distillate fuel	0.058	0.923	0.056	−1.318	0.114	0.022	0.022	0.022	0.022
Natural gas	0.058	0.325	0.056	0.256	−0.339	0.022	0.022	0.022	0.022
Kerosene	0.058	0.154	0.056	0.256	0.114	−0.108	0.022	0.022	0.022
Still gas	0.058	0.268	0.056	0.256	0.114	0.022	−0.667	0.022	0.022
Liquefied petroleum gas	0.058	0.168	0.056	0.256	0.114	0.022	0.022	−1.238	0.022
Petroleum coke	0.058	0.018	0.056	0.256	0.114	0.022	0.022	0.022	−4.448

computed from a simulation that is solved dynamically from 1955 through 1972, an average error of 10 percent between the actual and simulated values is rather small. In fact, electricity, natural gas, and coal, which account for 82.7 percent of average fuel demands, have an error of less than 6 percent. The reader is reminded that the model includes only fuel and power demands, and thus petrochemical feedstocks, metallurgical coal, and other raw material uses are excluded.

Household-Commercial Sector. The HHC simulations were somewhat better than the industrial sector simulations. None of the MAEs is more than 10 percent of the series means. Natural gas, distillate, and electricity have errors that are less than 6 percent. These three fuels constitute more than 80 percent of the total fuel demand in the HHC sector, and they have a total cumulative error of less than 6 percent.

Elasticities

From the estimated logit regressions we can compute short run and long run demand elasticities with respect to changes in the price of each fuel. While the own-price elasticities for each fuel are different, the cross-price elasticities are invariant with respect to the denominator of the estimated logit regression. The proof for this property appears in Appendix 2A. The short run own and cross elasticities for each fuel are presented in Tables 2–10 and 2–11 for the IND and HHC sectors, respectively. The long run own and cross elasticities are presented in Tables 2–12 and 2–13.

Industrial Sector. While all of the own and cross elasticities are of the correct sign, three things should be pointed out. First, for any given price the cross elasticities are identical except in the case of the price of coal. This is a property of the logit formulation and is proven in the appendix. Coal has different cross elasticities because it is the numeraire of the logit

Table 2–11
Short Run Own- and Cross-Price Elasticities: Household-Commercial Sector

Quantities	PELC	PBIT	PRF	PDF	PNG	PK	PLG
Electricity	−0.152	0.057	0.019	0.026	0.142	0.031	0.131
Anthracite coal	0.047	−0.587	0.019	0.026	0.142	0.031	0.131
Residual fuel	0.027	0.057	−0.019	0.026	0.142	0.031	0.131
Distillate fuel	−0.265	0.057	0.019	−0.345	0.142	0.031	0.131
Natural gas	0.072	0.057	0.019	0.026	−0.583	0.031	0.131
Kerosene	0.445	0.057	0.019	0.026	0.142	−0.926	0.131
Liquefied petroleum gas	−0.211	0.057	0.019	0.026	0.142	0.031	−0.298

Table 2-12
Long Run Own- and Cross-Price Elasticities: Industrial Sector

Quantities	PELC	PBIT	PRF	PDF	PNG	PK	PSG	PLG	PPC
Electricity	-1.635	0.395	0.115	0.101	0.852	0.208	0.208	0.208	0.208
Bituminous coal	0.118	-1.486	0.219	0.462	0.835	0.067	0.067	0.067	0.067
Residual fuel	0.118	2.126	-3.389	0.462	0.835	0.067	0.067	0.067	0.067
Distillate fuel	0.118	0.323	0.219	-1.763	0.835	0.067	0.067	0.067	0.067
Natural gas	0.118	0.272	0.219	0.462	-0.924	0.067	0.067	0.067	0.067
Kerosene	0.118	0.172	0.219	0.462	0.835	-0.111	0.067	0.067	0.067
Still gas	0.118	0.279	0.219	0.462	0.835	0.067	-1.189	0.067	0.067
Liquefied petroleum gas	0.118	0.941	0.219	0.462	0.835	0.067	0.067	-1.237	0.067
Petroleum coke	0.118	0.049	0.219	0.462	0.835	0.067	0.067	0.067	-0.840

Prices

Table 2-13
Long Run Own- and Cross-Price Elasticities: Household-Commercial Sector

	Prices						
Quantities	PELC	PBIT	PRF	PDF	PNG	PK	PLG
Electricity	−2.31	0.008	0.029	0.342	1.281	0.104	0.041
Anthracite coal	−1.57	−0.720	0.029	0.342	1.281	0.104	0.041
Residual fuel	−1.68	0.008	−0.602	0.342	1.281	0.104	0.041
Distillate fuel	0.037	0.008	0.029	−2.00	1.281	0.104	0.041
Natural gas	1.642	0.008	0.029	0.342	−2.667	0.104	0.041
Kerosene	3.890	0.008	0.029	0.342	1.281	−6.062	0.041
Liquefied petroleum gas	−1.024	0.008	0.029	0.342	1.281	0.104	−1.243

regression. Second, the cross elasticities for kerosene, still gas, liquefied petroleum gas, and petroleum coke are identical because the same price was used for the four fuels (as mentioned in note c). Third, normally we would believe a priori that the price elasticity of demand should become larger as we move from the short run to the long run. This is not true in all instances if we compare Tables 2–10 and 2–12. While some own elasticities (electricity and liquefied petroleum gas) declined in the long run, distillate fuel was the only cross elasticity for a major fuel that experienced a decline in the long run. The explanation for some of the decline could be attributed to the model formulation that is a hierarchy computation. An increase in the price of any fuel not only influences the price of that fuel, but influences the split between electricity and fossil fuels through its weighted average price and the total demand for fuel for industry via its weighted average in *TOTPR*.

Household-Commercial Sector. In the household-commercial sector all the own and cross elasticities are of the correct sign except for electricity. This curious effect of negative cross elasticities with respect to the price of electricity could be due to the fact that the logit regressions are normalized with respect to electricity. However, this phenomenon did not appear in the industrial sector when the logit regressions were normalized with respect to bituminous coal. Other than the unexplained negative cross elasticities with respect to electricity prices, the own and cross elasticities appear to be of the correct sign and magnitude. All own and cross elasticities increased in moving from the long run to the short run except for coal, which would be expected because the demand for coal in the HHC sector has been declining since 1948.

Conclusions

In summary we can say that fuel substitution possibilities do exist in the IND and HHC sectors. A price increase of any one fuel should induce a decline in demand for that fuel while stimulating the demand for its substitute. Because the cross elasticities are nonzero, there appear to be fuel substitution possibilities between electricity and the fossil fuels. Last, since the negative own elasticities are larger than the cross elasticities, a price increase in all fuels in any sector will not increase the total demand for energy in that sector.

References

[1] Fair, Ray C. "An Evaluation of a Short Run Forecasting Model." *International Economic Review* 15, no. 2 (June 1974): 285–303.

[2] Federal Energy Administration. *Project Independence Report*. Washington, D.C.: U.S. Government Printing Office, 1974.

[3] Griffin, James M. "The Effects of Higher Prices on Electricity Consumption." *Bell Journal of Economics and Management Science* 5, no. 2 (Autumn 1974): 515–539.

[4] Hausman, Jerry A. "Project Independence Report: An Appraisal of U.S. Energy Needs Up to 1985." *Bell Journal of Economics and Management Science* 6, no. 2 (Autumn 1975): 517–551.

[5] Kennedy, Michael. "An Econometric Model of the World Oil Market." *Bell Journal of Economics and Management Science* 5, no. 2 (Autumn 1974): 540–577.

[6] Kraft, John, and Arthur Kraft. "Empirical Estimation of the Value of Travel Time Using Multi-Mode Choice Models." *Journal of Econometrics* 2, no. 4 (December 1974): 317–326.

[7] ———. "Interfuel Substitution and Energy Consumption in the Industrial Sector." Mimeographed, Washington, D.C., 1975.

[8] MacAvoy, Paul W., and Roger Noll. "Relative Prices on Regulated Transactions of the Natural Gas Pipelines." *Bell Journal of Economics and Management Science* 4, no. 1 (Spring 1973): 212–234.

[9] McFadden, Daniel. "Conditional Logit Analysis of Qualitative Choice Behavior." In Paul Zarembka, ed., *Frontiers in Econometrics*. New York: Academic Press, 1974.

[10] Nerlove, Mark, and S.J. Press. "Univariate and Multivariate Log-Linear and Logistic Models." Santa Monica: Rand Corporation, 1973.

[11] Schmidt, Peter, and Richard P. Strauss. "The Prediction of Occupation Using Multiple Logit Models." *International Economic Review* 16, no. 2 (June 1975): 471–486.

[12] Theil, Henri. "A Multinomial Extension of the Linear Logit Model." *International Economic Review* 10, no. 3 (October 1969): 251–259.

Appendix 2A

Assume the dependent variable of the logit regression is a share ratio (S_i/S_j) where the shares are constrained such that

$$\sum_{\substack{i=1 \\ i=j}}^{n} S_i = 1 \quad \text{and} \quad 0 < S_i < 1.$$

The independent variables are the price ratio (P_i/P_j) and the lagged share ratio. If Q_{tot} is equal to the sum of the quantities $Q_j, j = 1, \ldots, n$ associated with the shares S_j, then the relative share ratios are functions of relative prices and

$$Q_{tot} = \sum_{j=1}^{n} Q_j$$

$$\frac{S_1}{S_n} = f\left(\frac{P_1}{P_n}\right)$$

$$\frac{S_2}{S_n} = f\left(\frac{P_2}{P_n}\right)$$

$$\frac{S_{n-1}}{S_n} = f\left(\frac{P_{n-1}}{P_n}\right)$$

The absolute quantities Q_j, having already solved for S_n, are

$$Q_n(P_1, \ldots, P_n) = Q_n(P) = S_n * Q_{tot}$$

$$Q_1(P_1, \ldots, P_n) = Q_n(P) * \left(\frac{S_1}{S_n}\right) = Q_n(P) * f\left(\frac{P_1}{P_n}\right)$$

$$Q_2(P_1, \ldots, P_n) = Q_n(P) * \left(\frac{S_2}{S_n}\right) = Q_n(P) * f\left(\frac{P_2}{P_n}\right)$$

$$\cdot \quad \cdot \quad \cdot$$

$$Q_{n-1}(P_1, \ldots, P_n) = Q_n(P) * \left(\frac{S_{n-1}}{S_n}\right) = Q_n(P) * f\left(\frac{P_{n-1}}{P_n}\right)$$

Then for $j = 1, \ldots, n - 1$, the new quantity Q_j, due to a change in price, $P_i, i \neq j$, yields:

$$\frac{\Delta Q_j}{Q_j} \simeq \frac{\acute{Q}_j - Q_j}{\frac{1}{2}(\acute{Q}_j + Q_j)} = \frac{\acute{Q}_n(P) * f\left(\frac{P_j}{P_n}\right) - Q_n(P) * f\left(\frac{P_j}{P_n}\right)}{\frac{1}{2}\left(\acute{Q}_n(P) * f\left(\frac{P_j}{P_n}\right) + Q_n(P) * f\left(\frac{P_j}{P_n}\right)\right)},$$

and by rearranging the above we get

$$\frac{\Delta Q_j}{Q_j} = \frac{\acute{Q}_n(P) - Q_n(P)}{\frac{1}{2} * (\acute{Q}_n(P) + Q_n(P))},$$

which is independent of j. Thus the cross elasticity of Q_j with respect to price P_i, $i \neq j$ is independent of j and invariant with i. For the own elasticity the quantity change Q_i, due to a change in price P_i, gives

$$\frac{\Delta Q_i}{Q_i} = \frac{\acute{Q}_i - Q_i}{\frac{1}{2} * (\acute{Q}_i + Q_i)} = \frac{\acute{Q}_n(P) * f\left(\frac{\acute{P}_i}{P_n}\right) - Q_n(P) * f\left(\frac{P_i}{P_n}\right)}{\frac{1}{2} * \left(\acute{Q}_n(P) * f\left(\frac{\acute{P}_i}{P_n}\right) + Q_n(P) * f\left(\frac{P_i}{P_n}\right)\right)}$$

with $i = 1, \ldots, n$. Thus the own elasticity is different from the cross elasticity.

We should note that three levels of elasticities may be computed. Let S_i = share of the ith energy input in a given sector; D_i = total demand for the ith energy input in a given sector; and T = total energy in that sector.

The system elasticity reflects a change in demand for input i in response to a change in the price of j. However, the change in price j induces two responses in the system: a change in the total demand for energy in the sector and a change in the share of i within the sector. Thus the system elasticity is:

$$\begin{pmatrix} \text{system} \\ \text{elasticity} \end{pmatrix} = \begin{pmatrix} \text{share} \\ \text{elasticity} \end{pmatrix} + \begin{pmatrix} \text{total} \\ \text{elasticity} \end{pmatrix},$$

which can be proved readily since

$$S_i = \frac{Q_i}{Q_{tot}} \quad \text{or} \quad Q_i = S_i * Q_{tot}$$

and

$$\frac{\partial Q_i}{\partial P_j} \cdot \frac{P_j}{Q_i} = \left(\frac{\partial S_i}{\partial P_j} * Q_{tot} + \frac{\partial Q_{tot}}{\partial P_j} * S_i\right) * \frac{P_j}{Q_i}$$

$$= \frac{\partial S_i}{\partial P_j} * \frac{P_j}{S_i} + \frac{\partial Q_{tot}}{\partial P_j} * \frac{P_j}{Q_{tot}}.$$

3

The Capital Stock Adjustment Process and the Demand for Gasoline: A Market-Share Approach*

Derriel Cato, Mark Rodekohr, and James Sweeney

Introduction

Numerous automobile gasoline consumption models have been developed in response to recent and ongoing petroleum production and import conditions. Most studies have estimated gasoline demand using various forms of a flow adjustment model.[1] The basic form of this model expresses gasoline consumption as a function of the real price of gasoline, disposal income, and gasoline consumption in the previous period. A model so structured only implicitly captures the stock dynamics that lead to changes in the average efficiency of the stock of automobiles over time via changes in the market shares of large and small cars.

Very few studies have explored the determination of the market share or the demand for cars by class. The Sweeney, Rand, and Chase studies deal with this market share problem, all using distinctly different methodologies. Sweeney uses one equation to estimate the new car sales-weighted miles per gallon as a function of the price of gas and a technology factor. The Rand study estimates the miles per gallon of the stock of automobiles as a function of the price of gas and other variables. The Chase study estimates the demand for cars by class with the use of a variety of functional forms and variables.[2] This chapter attempts to model the market shares of small, medium, and large cars with the use of commodity hierarchy theory, which provides a consistent specification for the demand equations. Then using the estimated shares of classes of cars and estimates of vehicle miles, we determine gasoline consumption. While the results are not entirely satisfactory, they provide a well-developed framework for future analysis.

This chapter is organized into four sections. The first section develops a hedonic classification system that separates automobiles into three classes based on the curb weight and brake horsepower of each domestic and imported make and model. Using the quantities of small, medium, and large cars generated by the hedonic classification, the second section develops a set of demand equations that represent a model for each market class based on prices, income, and the lagged stock of automobiles. In the second section we also examine the demand functions to determine whether they characterize a commodity hierarchy. The third section uses the demand functions estimated in the second section to produce estimates of the sales of small, medium, and large cars. This estimation is done using a normalization scheme. The final part of the third section develops a gasoline demand model and then presents the appropriate price, income, and technology elasticities. The conclusion summarizes the results and presents a brief discussion of the policy implications.

Hedonic Classification

To specify the demands for various classes of automobiles it is necessary to develop a consistent classification system. Other studies of automobile demand by class of automobile—such as the work by Chase Econometrics and Transportation Systems Center—have used the industrial classification system. But the industrial system classifies cars only on the basis of wheelbase; it ignores other factors.

We define *class* to be any grouping of commodities that is relatively homogenous. The homogeneity is determined by the set of attributes or characteristics that are embodied in each make and model of cars within each class.

The theoretical basis for the proposed scheme is based on the work of Kelvin Lancaster, who, among others, has argued that the demand for a commodity is based on the demand for attributes of the specific product.[3] We develop a hedonic classification system that classifies automobiles on the basis of a certain set of characteristics embodied in each make and model of car. This system is a modification of the hedonic price index developed by Griliches. The hedonic scheme is based on the empirical hypothesis that a commodity can usefully be viewed as an aggregate of individual characteristics. However, in our work we assume that differences in characteristics represent distinctly different quality levels. For example, a commodity A embodied with a large quantity of characteristics represents a quality level superior to that of a commodity B that has lesser amounts of the same characteristics. We assume further that these quality levels are ranked into preference orderings by consumers. Therefore commodity A is ranked at a higher preference ordering than commodity B, and A is not viewed as being merely a larger amount of commodity B.

The hedonic price index is commonly used as a method of accounting for "pure price changes" or changes in prices not associated with any change in quality over time.[4] We are not concerned with price changes over time but rather with quantity changes over time in a specific quality level. Therefore we use changes in the characteristic mix over a time as the basis for observing changes in quantities over time. This implies a system in which cars are classified in homogenous classes on the basis of differences in the characteristic mix of each class of car. These classes represent the previously mentioned quality levels.

Therefore slightly modifying the work of Griliches,[5] we express the log of the price (ln $P_{i,t}$) of the ith make and model in year t as a function of the log of the vector of characteristics of the ith make and model in year t (ln $X_{i,t}$)

$$\ln P_{i,t} = \beta^* \ln X_{i,t}. \qquad (3.1)$$

Following this theoretical formulation it is necessary to specify the characteristic set associated with the particular product. A car, for example, has an almost infinite possible set of characteristics. Therefore it is necessary to specify some subset of the possible characteristic set that could adequately explain significant differences between classes of the commodity. As one would expect, this type of classification scheme inherently embodies multicollinearity problems, which by definition could lead to the estimation of unstable parameters.

Therefore, with this constraint in mind, we chose a characteristic set that has stable parameter estimates and at the same time was a reasonable approximation of the attributes of the product. For these reasons we chose weight ($W_{i,t}$) and horsepower ($HP_{i,t}$) of the ith make and model in year t. The weight variable represents a proxy for luxury characteristics, and horsepower is a proxy for performance. Various combinations of weight and horsepower with other characteristics such as length, wheelbase, and interior capacity were estimated; but the coefficients were either unstable or had the wrong sign, a result of their multicollinearity with weight. A necessary condition of Eq. (3.1) is that the coefficient of any attribute have a positive sign. A negative sign would imply that greater quantities of any characteristic cause a decrease in price, which violates the assumptions previously stated.

Data on curb weights, brake horsepowers, and sticker prices of domestic makes and models from the almanac issues of *Automotive News* are used to estimate Eq. (3.2). The parameter values of Eq. (3.2) are then used to classify all other years, makes, and models into either small, medium, or large cars based on the index generated with Eq. (3.3).

$$\ln P_{i,1971} = 1.89 + 1.03 * \ln(W_{i,1971})$$
$$(9.2)$$

$$+ 0.32 \ln(HP_{i,1971}) \qquad (3.2)$$
$$(4.4)$$

$$\bar{R}^2 = 0.79$$

(*t*-values are in parentheses).

Figure 3–1 illustrates this partitioning method. The solid lines in this figure were estimated to make cars in one class as price-homogenous as possible.

$$\begin{array}{ll} \textit{Index} & \textit{Class} \\ (P_{i,t}) < 3550 & \text{small} \\ 3551 < (P_{i,t}) < 5250 & \text{medium} \\ (P_{i,t}) > 5251 & \text{large} \end{array} \quad (3.3)$$

This system classifies cars into the three classes on the basis of 1971 equivalents. Therefore the quantity of small cars in 1969 is actually the quantity of 1971 equivalent cars in 1969. This methodology is employed to abstract from changes in technology that have affected the average weight of all cars over time. For purposes of analysis in the next section, we placed all imported cars into the small class. Previous analysis using the hedonic technique indicates that this introduces very little bias into the classification process. We found from previous results that almost all imports fall into the small class with less than 5 percent of total imports falling into the medium and large classes in any given year.

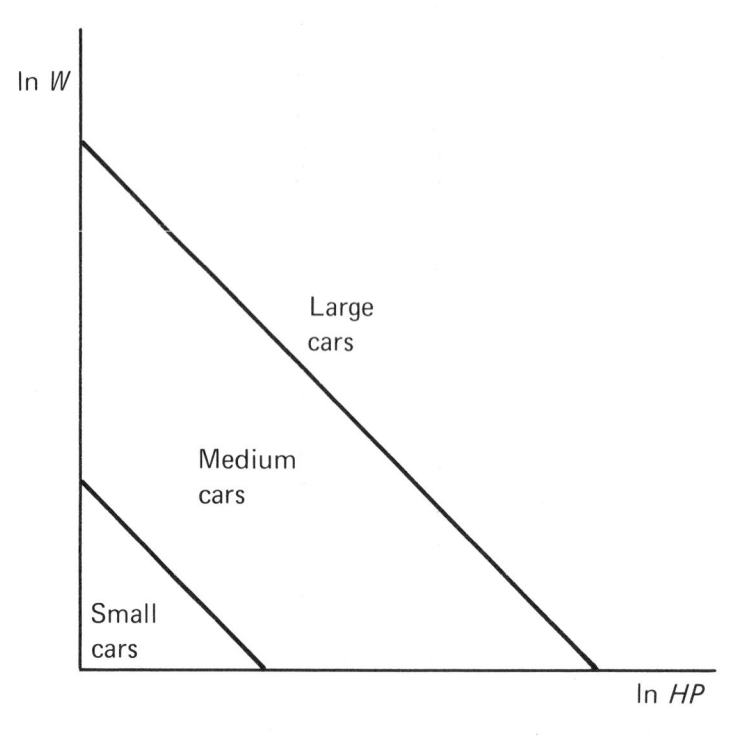

Figure 3–1. Partitioned Automobile Class.

Table 3-1
Parameter Estimates of Hedonic Equation over Time

Year	Constant β_0	Weight β_1	Horsepower β_3	$\bar{R}^2$
1973	−1.50 (−1.5)	1.02 (6.0)	0.26 (2.27)	0.77
1971	−1.89 (−2.8)	1.03 (9.2)	0.32 (4.4)	0.79
1969	−2.10 (−2.2)	1.06 (7.0)	0.27 (3.7)	0.75
1967	−3.90 (−3.5)	1.40 (8.02)	0.09 (1.2)	0.77
1965	−1.26 (−1.29)	0.94 (5.7)	0.33 (3.18)	0.77
1963	−4.37 (−3.13)	1.50 (6.7)	0.009 (0.09)	0.74
1961	−1.03 (−0.88)	0.97 (5.1)	0.22 (2.5)	0.77
1959	−1.10 (−0.73)	0.94 (3.86)	0.26 (2.1)	0.68

Note: Numbers in parentheses are *t*-statistics.

To explore the stability of Eq. (3.2) over time, we estimated an identical equation for the years 1973, 1969, 1967, 1965, 1963, 1961, and 1959.[a] Table 3-1 summarizes the results of this analysis. It is clear that the coefficients are extremely stable over time with the weight coefficient equal to approximately 1.0 and centering around the values 1.06 and 0.94. The coefficient on horsepower is less stable and approximately equals 0.25. One reason for this stable behavior is that almost any attribute that we have not included in these equations is associated with the weight variable. Therefore variations in the weight component embody many other luxury characteristics.

The Demand for New Cars by Class of Car

Commodity Hierarchy Specification

Following the derivation of the quantities of small, medium, and large cars, we present the demand equations for these cars. The theoretical

---
[a]It would be desirable to perform a Chow test on the coefficients; however, our computer program would not allow us to input the necessary amount of observations.

basis for the demand functions are based on the assumed existence of a commodity hierarchy.

Commodity hierarchy theory presupposes the presence of a commodity class characterized by "ranked" quality levels, and it is viewed as an extension of received consumer theory under conditions related to consumer choice within a commodity class.[6] Given the demand for a commodity, the particular element of the commodity class chosen will depend upon relative prices within the commodity class. Strictly interpreted, only relative prices between adjacent quality levels enter the choice calculus. A change in the price of a large car does not affect the demand for small cars, whereas the demand for medium cars could change.

Before turning to the statistical results, we will contrast the a priori demand structure of a commodity hierarchy with received theory. In all the a priori specifications, the own derivatives are negative and the cross derivatives are nonnegative, therefore:

Q_i = the quantity demanded of the ith quality level or product where $i = 1, \ldots, j, \ldots, n$;
P_i = the price of the ith level;
α_j, δ_j = the own or cross partials.

Condition I may be written as:

$$\frac{\partial Q_i}{\partial P_j} = \alpha_j \leq 0 \quad i = j$$

Condition I

$$\frac{\partial Q_i}{\partial P_j} = \delta_j \geq 0 \quad i \neq j.$$

The received theory does not restrict the magnitude of the cross derivatives, whereas the hierarchy theory requires that the cross derivatives be no larger than the own derivatives. This is expressed as Condition II:

$$\sum_{j=1}^{i} \frac{\partial Q_i}{\partial P_j} \leq 0 \quad \text{for all } i. \quad \text{Condition II}$$

Condition II states that an increase in the price of the ith class will always result in a decrease (or no change) in total quantity demanded under the hierarchy assumptions. The last necessary condition for the existence of a commodity hierarchy is that the nonadjacent class derivatives equal zero; this is expressed as Condition III:

$$\frac{\partial Q_i}{\partial P_j} = 0 \quad \text{if } i > j + 1 \text{ or } i < j - 1. \quad \text{Condition III}$$

Empirical Demand Functions

Using the a priori specification suggested by commodity hierarchy theory, we now develop the empirical demand functions used in the model. Using the estimated functions, we then test for the existence of a commodity hierarchy. The only a priori restriction placed on these functions corresponds to Condition III, which excludes the nonadjacent class prices from the class demand functions.[b]

We use the quantities of small, medium, and large cars (Q_s, Q_m, and Q_L) derived from the hedonic classification system to specify the specific demand functions. Letting $NPOP_t$ represent total population, CPI_t represent the consumer price index, STK_t represent the total stock of all cars, YDN_t represent real disposable income, and $GP_{s,t}$, $GP_{m,t}$, and $GP_{L,t}$ represent the generalized price of small, medium, and large cars, respectively, in year t, we construct Eqs. (3.4), (3.5), and (3.6).[7]

$$(Q_{s,t}/NPOP_t) = f[(GP_{s,t}/CPI_t), \quad (GP_{m,t}/CPI_t), \\ (YDN_t), \quad (STK_{t-1}/NPOP_{t-1})] \quad (3.4)$$

$$(Q_{m,t}/NPOP_t) = f[(GP_{s,t}/CPI_t), \quad (GP_{m,t}/CPI_t), \\ (GP_{L,t}/CPI_t), \quad (YDN_t), \quad (STK_{t-1}/NPOP_{t-1})] \quad (3.5)$$

$$(Q_{L,t}/NPOP_t) = f[(GP_{m,t}/CPI_t), \quad (GP_{L,t}/CPI_t), \\ (YDN_t), \quad (STK_{t-1}/NPOP_{t-1})]. \quad (3.6)$$

The generalized price used in these functions consists of two elements—the sticker price and the total discounted gasoline cost associated with each class of car. Therefore the generalized price of cars in a class c (GP_c) is expressed as a function of the sticker price (P_c), discount rate r (which is assumed to equal 10 percent), average new car miles per gallon in each class (MPG_c), price of gasoline ($PGAS$), and vehicle miles per year (VM), which is assumed to be constant across class and equal to 10,000 miles per year. Equation (3.7) summarizes the determination of the generalized price.[8]

$$GP_c = P_c + \sum_{i=0}^{9} \frac{(PGAS/MPG_c) * VM_i}{(1 + r)^i}. \quad (3.7)$$

---

[b]Two additional sets of demand functions were also estimated. The first set expressed the quantity demanded of each class as a function of the prices of all classes of autos and other variables. The second set expressed the quantity demanded of each class as a function of the own price and no other prices, and other exogenous variables. The results of these two sets of estimated demand functions were unreliable because the price variables contained many incorrect signs and insignificant *t*-statistics.

These demand functions implicitly assume that consumers correctly discount the lifetime gasoline costs associated with the operation of each class of car. The total stock variable is constructed assuming exponential scrappage. Specifically, this is the total stock that is a function of last year's stock and current new car sales (*NCS*).

$$STK_t = NCS_t + 0.92 * STK_{t-1}$$

where (3.8)

$$NCS_t = Q_{s,t} + Q_{m,t} + Q_{L,t}.$$

The annual scrappage rate is assumed to equal 8 percent.[9]

Each demand equation includes the lagged per capita total stock of cars. This assumption is necessary because even though commodity hierarchy theory assumes that all consumers have identical preference orderings of commodity classes based on quality levels, consumers adjust their demand on the basis of additions to the total stock of a given good; i.e., given the decision to purchase a car, hierarchy theory provides a basis for the choice of the class of car that is purchased. The consumers, however, still maximize utility on the basis of their total holding of cars. This assumption is particularly useful in the case of automobiles because many consumer units own not only more than one car but more than one class of car.

Using the seemingly unrelated generalized least squares (GLS) regression technique developed by Zellner, Eqs. (3.4), (3.5), and (3.6) are estimated jointly.[10] The results of these regressions appear in Table 3–2. Using these demand functions, we can now examine the existence of a commodity hierarchy.

It is clear that Condition I is met; all the own derivatives are negative and all cross derivates are positive. However, Condition II is not met because the elasticity of the total quantity with respect to a change in any price is positive for the medium class (see the last column of Table 3–2). Even if Condition III is not imposed on the demand equations (i.e., all prices enter the equations), previous analysis indicates that both Conditions I and II are violated. We therefore conclude that the demand for automobiles cannot conform to the specifications required in a commodity hierarchy. This result probably occurred because mutual exclusivity of each class of automobile is a necessary assumption for hierarchy theory. This assumption as well as others allows identical preference rankings by consumers. The purchase of more than one class by the consuming unit violates the necessary mutual exclusivity assumptions.

However, by estimating the demand for all new cars and using a normalization scheme, one can use the demand equations summarized in

Table 3–2
Estimated Demand Equations for Small, Medium, and Large Cars

(Logarithmic) Independent Variable	(Logarithmic) Dependent Variable $Q_s/NPOP$	$Q_m/NPOP$	$Q_L/NPOP$	$\left(\dfrac{P_j}{\sum_{i=1}^{3} Q_i}\right) \sum_{i=1}^{3} \dfrac{\partial Q_i}{\partial P_j}$
GP_s	−2.16 (−4.98)	0.25 (1.6)		−0.36
GP_m	6.72 (6.81)	−0.96 (−1.3)	0.51 (0.4)	+0.93
GP_L		1.13 (2.24)	−2.1 (−2.44)	−0.11
$YD58/NPOP$	6.74 (3.34)	5.2 (8.9)	8.53 (8.5)	
$STK_{-1}/NPOP_{-1}$	−7.31 (−2.67)	−3.72 (−1.46)	−8.24 (−2.11)	
Constant	1.53	17.09	57.86	
$\bar{R}^2$	0.88	0.88	0.90	
D.W.	3.29	2.4	2.62	

Note: Numbers in parentheses are *t*-statistics.

Table 3–2 to produce a workable set of demand equations that in turn can be used to explore the effects of higher gasoline prices, changes in technology, and changes in other environmental variables.

A Market-Share Gasoline Demand Model

The Market-Share Model

Using the demand equations summarized in Table 3–2 and a normalization process, we can now develop a model that predicts the market shares of small, medium, and large cars in response to changes in critical policy variables such as the price of gasoline, taxes on inefficient cars, and changes in technology. First, an equation that estimates the demand for total new cars is estimated. To estimate the total new car demand it is necessary to develop a measure of aggregate prices for new cars. Because the market class equations are based on the prices of each class of cars, the aggregate price used is a quantity-weighted index that is composed of the generalized prices of small, medium, and large cars and the corresponding lagged quantities. This aggregate price variable is summarized in Eq. (3.9), where GTP_t represents the aggregate price of all new cars.

$$GTP_t = \sum_i GP_i * Q_{i,t-1} / \sum_i Q_{i,t-1} \qquad (3.9)$$

where

$i = $ small, medium, and large cars.

Lagged quantities are used to keep the system recursive; therefore problems of simultaneity are avoided.[c] The aggregate new car equation is a dynamic stock adjustment equation where the per capita demand for new cars is a function of the real aggregate generalized price, real disposable income per capita, and last period's per capita stock of cars. Using ordinary least squares, Eq. (3.10) summarizes the results of this estimation. The price and stock variables have the expected negative signs and the income coefficient is positive.

$$\begin{aligned} NCS = \ & NPOP * EXP(30.86 - 1.84 * \ln(GTP/CPI) \\ & \hspace{7em} (-8.02) \\ & + \ 1.967 * \ln(YD58/NPOP) \\ & \hspace{3em} (4.91) \\ & - \ 2.33 * \ln(PCR/NPOP) \\ & \hspace{3em} (-4.62) \end{aligned} \qquad (3.10)$$

$$\bar{R}^2 = 0.76; \quad D.W. = 1.5.$$

Normalization Process

Following the determination of new-car sales from Eq. (3.10), the nonnormalized quantities of small, medium, and large cars (NQ_s, NQ_m, NQ_L) are estimated with Eqs. (3.4), (3.5), and (3.6). The simple normalization process outlined in Eqs. (3.11) and (3.12) produces estimates of the quantities of small, medium, and large cars demanded.

$$TNQ_t = \sum_i NQ_{t,i} \qquad (3.11)$$

$$Q_{t,i} = (NQ_{t,i}/TNQ_t) * NCS_t \qquad (3.12)$$

where $i = $ small, medium, and large cars.

---

[c]The lagged quantity is also used to partially adjust for the difference between the model year in which autos are commonly sold and the calendar that is used in the analysis.

This normalization process converts the nonnormalized quantities into shares that must sum to one; therefore the sum of the normalized quantities must equal the total new car sales produced by Eq. (3.10).

Following the estimation of the quantities of each class of car, the sales-weighted miles per gallon of new cars can be derived easily. The sales-weighted miles per gallon is a quantity-weighted average of the gallon per mile (GPM) of each class of cars. Using average gallons per mile is equivalent to taking the harmonic mean of miles per gallon, which is necessary to preserve the proper units. Equation (3.13) expresses the determination of the new car sales-weighted miles per gallon (MPG) in period t.

$$MPG_t = \frac{(\sum_i Q_{t,i} * GPM_{t,i})}{NCS_t}. \qquad (3.13)$$

The final component of the stock adjustment process involves the calculation of the sales-weighted miles per gallon of the stock of autos ($AMPG_t$) in period t. Assuming exponential scrappage and usage rates, Eq. (3.14) represents the capital stock vintage process. Specifically, the average miles per gallon of the stock in any period t ($AMPG_t$) is a function of last period's adjusted stock (PCR), the scrappage rate (δ), the usage rate (γ), and the quantity and miles per gallon of new cars:

$$AMPG_t = \frac{[NCS_t/MPG_t + (\delta * \gamma * PCR_{t-1})/AMPG_{t-1}]}{PCR_t}. \qquad (3.14)$$

The adjusted stock refers to the stock that is adjusted for scrappage and utilization rates. The concept of adjusting the stock for relative usage was developed by James Sweeney in his paper the "Passenger Car Use of Gasoline" and refers to the fact that older cars are driven less. If new car sales are relatively small, the stock consists of older cars; therefore, assuming a declining utilization rate, the stock will be utilized less than if it consisted of many newer cars.[11]

The Determination of Vehicle Miles

Gasoline demand is not only a function of the efficiency of miles per gallon of the stock of cars but also a function of vehicle miles, or the amount of travel. Because the purpose of this chapter is to present a model of the capital stock adjustment process, we use an equation for vehicle miles that was developed by James Sweeney. Sweeney uses two equations that predict vehicle miles. The first one (3.15) estimates the cost of travel. This cost per mile (CPM_t) is a function of the passengers per car

(PC_t), a wage factor (WF_t) that adjusts the total wage rate for the proportion of wages valued in transportation, the wage rate (WR_t), the average speed of cars ($AVSP_t$), the price of gasoline ($PGAS_t$), and the average miles per gallon of the stock of cars ($AMPG_t$ from Eq. (3.14) in period t). Equation (3.15) expresses this relationship, which basically implies that the cost per mile of travel is a function of the opportunity cost and gasoline cost. Following the derivation of the cost component, Sweeney expresses

$$CPM_t \equiv \frac{(PC_t * WF_t * WR_t/CPI_t)}{AVSP_t} + \frac{(PGAS_t/CPI_t)}{AMPG_t}, \qquad (3.15)$$

vehicle miles (VM_t) per capita as a function of the cost per mile, income per capita, and the unemployment rate (RU_t). Using nonlinear least squares with a first-order autoregressive transformation, we estimated Eq. (3.16).[12]

$$VM_t = NPOP_t * EXP\ [6.518 + 0.80 * \ln(VM_{t-1}/NPOP_{t-1})$$
$$(12.13)\ \ (12.6)$$

$$- 0.3587 * \ln(CPM_t) + 0.98 * \ln(YD58_t/NPOP_t)$$
$$(-1.79) (11.15)$$

$$+ 0.0026 * RU - 0.81 * (6.518 +$$
$$(0.94) \qquad\qquad\qquad\qquad\qquad\qquad (3.16)$$

$$0.80 * \ln(VM_{t-2}/NPOP_{t-2}) - 0.3587 * (CPM_{t-1})$$

$$+ 0.98 * \ln(YD58_{t-1}/NPOP_{t-1})$$

$$+ 0.0026 * RU_{t-1})]$$

$$\bar{R}^2 = 0.996;\ \ \text{D.W.} = 1.13.$$

The final equation (3.17), expresses gasoline demand (GAS_t) in period t as an identity equal to vehicle miles divided by the average miles per gallon of the stock:

$$GAS_t \equiv VM_t/AMPG_t. \qquad (3.17)$$

Therefore gasoline demand changes in response to a change in vehicle miles and/or a change in the efficiency or average miles per gallon of the stock of cars.

In the short run the stock is relatively fixed; therefore most changes in gasoline demand are the result of changes in vehicle miles. In the long run, consumers can alter the efficiency of the stock, and thus long run gasoline demand changes are primarily due to changes in the average miles per gallon of the stock of cars.

Figure 3–2 illustrates the gasoline demand model presented in this section. The determination of the efficiency of the stock of cars in the long run is due to the market shares of small, medium, and large cars. The generalized price of these cars is a function of gasoline prices and sticker prices. The unnormalized small, medium, and large car demands are a function of the own-generalized prices in each class, the prices of cars in adjacent classes, and macroeconomic variables. Total new car demand is a function of the aggregate generalized price and macroeconomic variables. The normalization process determines the new car sales-weighted miles per gallon, and in turn affects the total new car demand in the following period by changing the quantity weights in the aggregate price equation. Through the vintaging process the new car miles per gallon changes the miles per gallon of the stock. The stock efficiency affects gasoline demand directly and through changes in the cost per mile, which in turn affects vehicle miles. Changes in technology, holding all other variables (such as new car prices) constant, alter gasoline demand through both changes in the average miles per gallon of the stock and the cost per mile.

In the short run, the response to an increase in gasoline prices is primarily made by reducing vehicle miles. In the long run, the adjustment to increases in gasoline prices is more complex. As gasoline prices increase, both the sales-weighted miles per gallon of new cars and the stock (at a much slower rate) increase. As the miles per gallon of the stock increases, the cost per mile decreases, holding gasoline prices constant; however, this increase in the stock miles per gallon was induced by increased gasoline prices. The net effect of the price increase on vehicle miles tends, in the long run, to hold total vehicle miles at the same level as before the price increase as consumers adjust by purchasing more efficient automobiles. Therefore, in total, the long run effect of higher gasoline prices is to reduce gasoline demand.

Elasticities

Using the model outlined in the previous section we now examine the various demand elasticities. We discuss the elasticities related to the normalized market shares, total new car sales, changes in technology, income, and changes in gasoline prices.

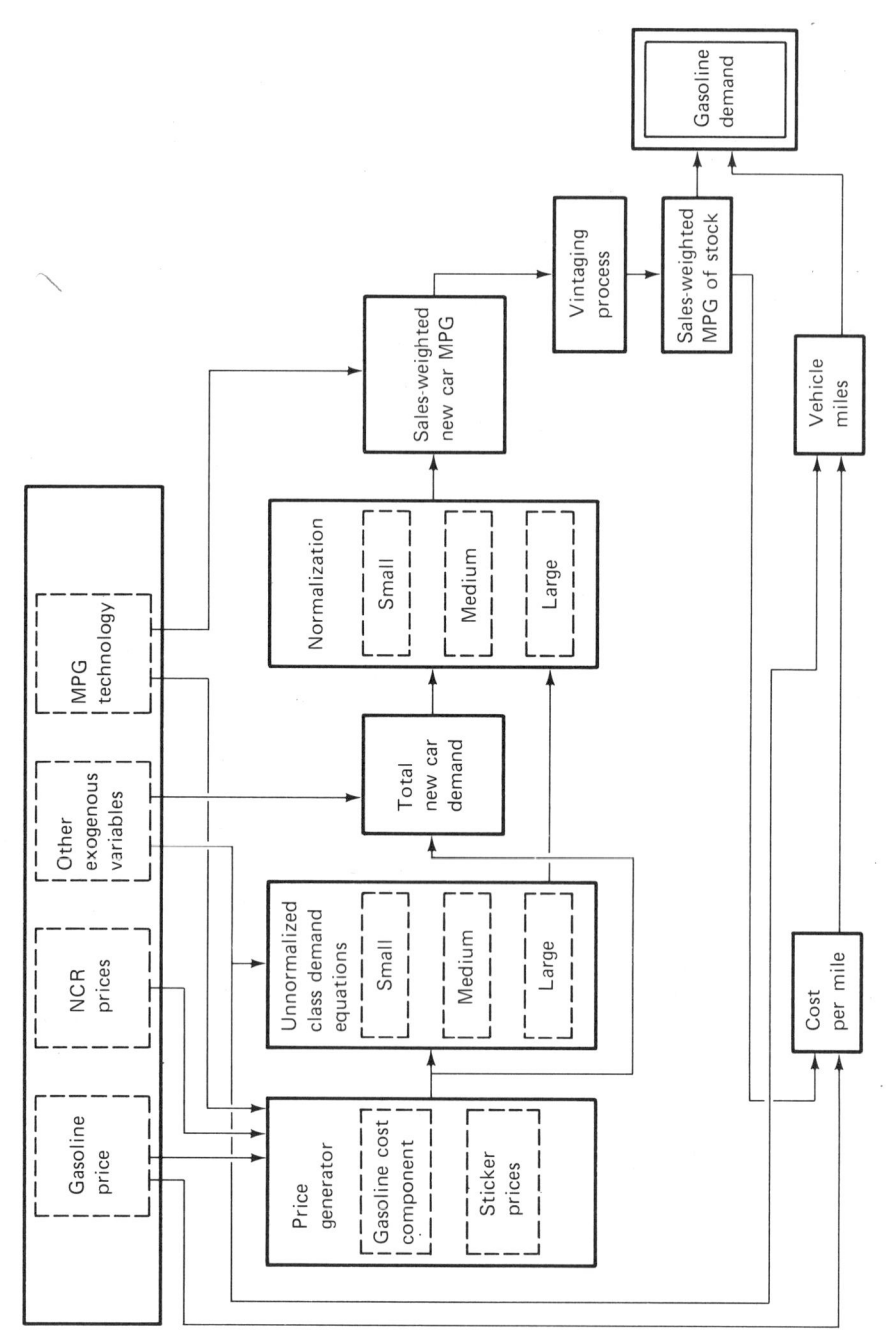

Figure 3-2. Flow Chart of Gasoline Demand Model.

Table 3–3 summarizes the normalized market-share own and cross elasticities. The first set of elasticities shows the changes in quantitues due to changes in the sticker prices of new cars. In all cases the one-year, or short run, elasticities are noted as SR and the twelve-year, or long run, elasticities are noted as LR. All the own sticker price elasticities are negative, with medium-sized cars being the most elastic and small cars being the most inelastic. All the cross elasticities are positive and relatively small with the following exceptions:

1. The cross elasticity of the quantity of small cars with respect to a change in medium car prices (η_{Q_s,P_m}) is positive but relatively large. This indicates that when consumers are faced with an increase in medium car prices, they are much more willing to move down in class than they are willing to move up in class when faced with an increase in small prices alone (since η_{Q_m,P_s} is much smaller than η_{Q_s,P_m}).
2. The cross elasticity of large cars with respect to a change in medium car prices is negative. This is due to the use of the normalization scheme since all the unnormalized elasticities have the correct sign.

Table 3–3
Market Share Elasticities

	η_{Q_s,P_s}	η_{Q_m,P_s}	η_{Q_L,P_s}
SR	−1.67	+0.312	+0.103
LR	−0.83	+0.213	+0.82

	η_{Q_s,P_m}	η_{Q_m,P_m}	η_{Q_L,P_m}
SR	+3.33	−2.67	−1.55
LR	+2.98	−1.73	−0.929

	η_{Q_s,P_L}	η_{Q_m,P_L}	η_{Q_L,P_L}
SR	−0.7	+0.185	−2.43
LR	−0.39	+0.268	−1.77

	η_{Q_s,GP_s}	η_{Q_m,GP_s}	η_{Q_L,GP_s}
SR	−1.99	+0.392	+0.14
LR	−1.49	+0.254	+0.82

	η_{Q_s,GP_m}	η_{Q_m,GP_m}	η_{Q_L,GP_m}
SR	+4.2	−3.47	−2.05
LR	+6.0	−2.13	−0.27

	η_{Q_s,GP_L}	η_{Q_m,GP_L}	η_{Q_L,GP_L}
SR	−0.89	+0.23	−2.94
LR	−0.72	+0.28	−2.74

3. The cross elasticity of small cars with respect to a change in large car prices is negative. Again this is due to the use of the normalization scheme.

The generalized price elasticities are identical to the sticker price elasticities except that they are higher in value. The reasons for the generalized negative cross price elasticities are the same as outlined previously.

All the total new car elasticities with respect to a change in the generalized price of each class (η_{NCR,GP_s}, η_{NCR,GP_m}, η_{NCR,GP_L}) are negative, and they illustrate that Condition II in the previous section is met. In other words, if the price of any class increases, total new car sales decrease. The short run total new car generalized price elasticity is initially high at -1.816, and it declines over time as the stock of cars adjusts. The long run generalized new car price elasticity equals -0.148. The short run new car elasticity is -0.385, whereas the long run elasticity is -0.125.

Table 3–4 summarizes the technology elasticities. The first row shows the changes in sales of small, medium, and large cars with respect to an increase in the miles per gallon of efficiency (*EFF*) of all classes of cars (and not an increase in the sales-weighted miles per gallon). An increase in the efficiency of all cars induces a shift from small cars to large cars since large cars are relatively cheaper after the increase in efficiency. The second row of elasticities shows the change in sales-weighted miles per gallon with respect to a change in the efficiency of small, medium, and

Table 3–4
Technology Elasticities

	$\eta_{Q_s,EFF}$	$\eta_{Q_m,EFF}$	$\eta_{Q_L,EFF}$
SR	-0.423	$+0.65$	$+0.97$
LR	-0.88	$+0.85$	$+1.12$

	η_{MPG,EFF_s}	η_{MPG,EFF_m}	η_{MPG,EFF_L}
SR	$+0.114$	$+0.924$	$+0.91$
LR	$+0.086$	$+1.078$	$+0.021$

	$\eta_{MPG,TP}$	$\eta_{MPG,TGP}$	$\eta_{MPG,PGAS}$
SR	$+0.401$	$+0.541$	$+0.131$
LR	$+0.429$	$+0.861$	$+0.31$

	$\eta_{MPG,EFF}$
SR	$+0.868$
LR	$+0.69$

large cars (η_{MPG,EFF_s}, η_{MPG,EFF_m}, η_{MPG,EFF_L}). As would be expected, all these elasticities are positive. The elasticity of new car sales-weighted miles per gallon with respect to a change in gasoline prices equals 0.135 in the short run and increases to equal 0.301 in the long run. The increase in the elasticity over time reflects the fact that consumers demand more smaller cars when faced with higher gasoline prices. The elasticity of new car sales-weighted miles per gallon with respect to a 1-percent increase in efficiency is less than one and equals 0.87 in the short run and 0.69 in the long run.[d] This elasticity does not equal one because if technology increases the efficiency of all cars, large- and medium-sized cars become relatively cheaper than smaller cars; therefore there is a shift toward larger cars and a corresponding decrease in MPG.

These results show that increasing efficiency of large cars will have a small effect on sales-weighted efficiency since there are two offsetting effects. First, those buying large cars will experience improved efficiency, and thus the sales-weighted efficiency improves. Offsetting this effect, however, is a market-share effect. This efficiency improvement will induce buyers to purchase more large cars and fewer small- and medium-sized cars. This effect reduces sales-weighted efficiency. The net result is only a small change in sales-weighted efficiency.

Table 3–5 summarizes the various income elasticities. The new car sales income elasticity is initially high at 1.97 and declines over time to equal 0.6 in the long run, as consumers adjust their relative purchases of large and small cars.

Table 3–6 summarizes the various gasoline elasticities. The price elasticity of gasoline equals −0.24 in the short run and −0.36 in the long run. The income elasticity equals 0.93 in the long run, whereas an increase in technology, which increases sales-weighted miles per gallon, equals −0.443 in the long run.

---

[d]In Sweeney, "Passenger Car Use of Gasoline," $\eta_{MPG,PGAS}$ equals 0.686 and $\eta_{MPG,EEF}$ equals 0.314. These results differ markedly from the results presented in this chapter. There is no evidence to indicate which result is correct.

Table 3–5
Income Elasticities

	$\eta_{Q_s,YDN}$	$\eta_{Q_m,YDN}$	$\eta_{Q_L,YDN}$
SR	+2.88	+1.32	+4.7
LR	+.2	+.662	+1.44

	$\eta_{NCR,YDN}$	$\eta_{MPG,YDN}$
SR	+1.977	+0.073
LR	+0.57	−0.055

Table 3–6
Gasoline Elasticities

	$\eta_{GAS,PGAS}$	$\eta_{GAS,EFF}$	$\eta_{GAS,YDN}$
SR	−0.244	−0.112	+0.16
LR	−0.363	−0.859	+0.933

	$\eta_{GAS,RMPG}$	$\eta_{GAS,TGP}$
SR	−0.072	−0.03
LR	−0.443	−0.553

In the final section, we use the model outlined to present several simulations of gasoline demand and new car sales. The simulations considered show a base case forecast as well as the effects of several types of policies on gasoline demand and new car sales.

Policy Simulations and Summary

Policy Simulations

To examine the effects on gasoline demand and other critical variables of several types of policies, we simulate the model for the years 1974 through 1985. Several assumptions are necessary before these simulations can be made. Using compound annual growth rates, we assume population to grow at a rate of 0.93 percent, real disposable income to grow at a rate of 2.58 percent, and the consumer price index to grow at a rate of 6.16 percent. Real gasoline prices are assumed to remain constant over time at their 1975 levels. The real sticker prices of small, medium, and large cars are assumed to remain constant at their 1973 levels.

Figures 3–3 through 3–6 illustrate the effects of a variety of possible policies on new car sales, new car sales-weighted miles per gallon, and gasoline demand. In other words, these figures illustrate the capital stock adjustment process that takes place in response to the various policies.

Four policies, all of which reduce gasoline demand, are analyzed. In all cases any reductions or increases in demand are in reference to changes relative to the base case. The first policy assumes that a $0.20 per gallon real (1975 dollars) gasoline tax is imposed. The policy decreases total new car sales but increases the sales of small cars while decreasing the sales of medium and large cars relative to the base case.

The second scenario assumes that a 20-percent increase in the efficiency of each class of cars is achieved without increasing the prices of cars. By 1985 this policy would cause the largest increase in new car

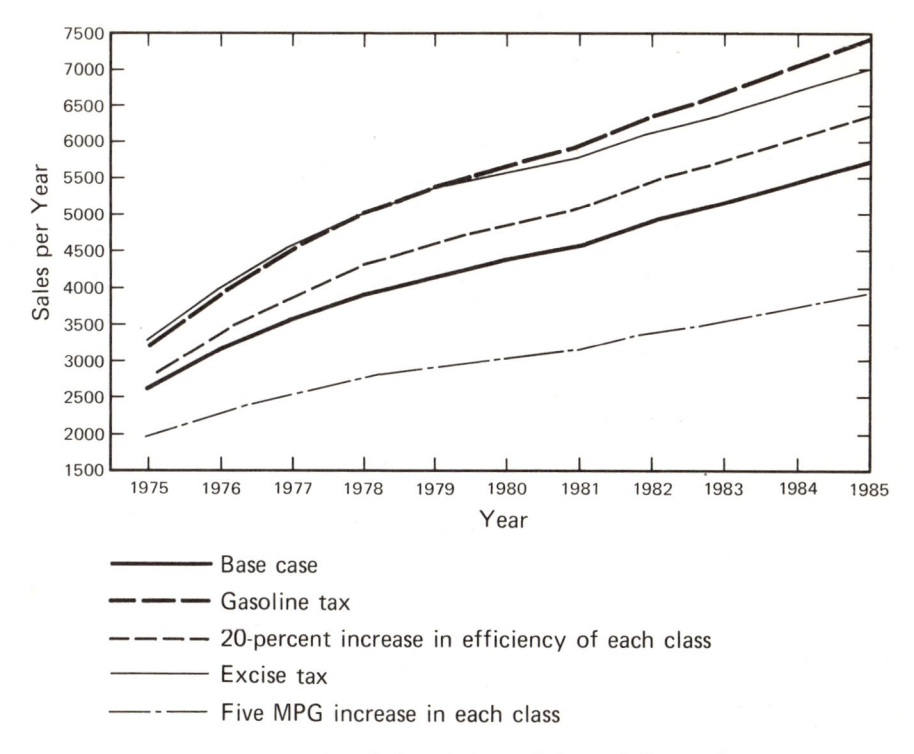

Figure 3–3. Small Car Sales—Selected Scenarios.

Legend:
— Base case
——— Gasoline tax
----- 20-percent increase in efficiency of each class
—— Excise tax
—·— Five MPG increase in each class

sales-weighted miles per gallon, and almost the greatest reduction in gasoline demand.

The next policy assumes that an excise tax is placed on inefficient cars. This policy assumes that on the average, large cars are taxed at $1000 per car, medium cars at $500 per car, and small cars at $250 per car. This tax is assumed to be real in nature and therefore to increase with the inflation rate. The effects of this tax are to decrease total new car sales. The sales of small cars would increase while medium and large car sales would decrease. This policy would reduce gasoline consumption but not by as much as any of the other policies.

The last scenario involves a policy that mandates an across-the-board increase of five miles per gallon in all classes of cars. Therefore the percentage increase in small car miles per gallon would be much lower than the percentage increase in large car miles per gallon. It is assumed that this policy would not be accompanied by any increase in new car prices. This policy would cause a slight increase in new car sales. The sales of small cars would decrease while the sales of medium and large cars would increase, due to the change in relative prices. This policy is

```
──────── Base case
─ ─ ─ ─  Gasoline tax
─ ─ ─ ─  20-percent increase in efficiency of each class
────────  Excise tax
─ · ─ · ─  Five MPG increase in each class
```

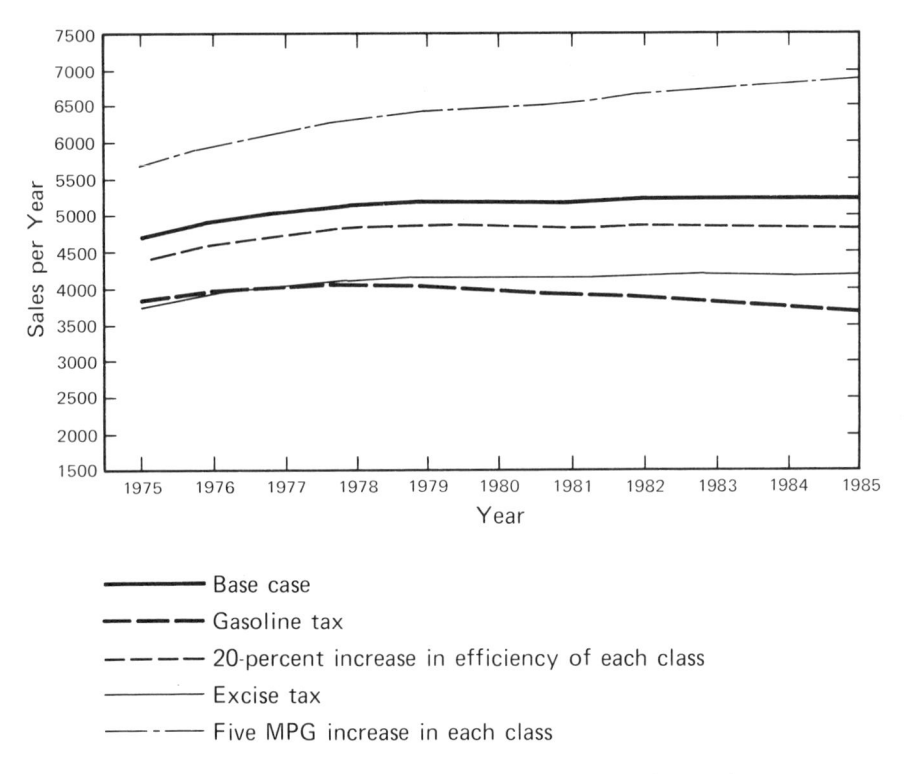

Figure 3-4. Medium Car Sales—Selected Scenarios.

associated with the second largest increase in new car sales-weighted miles per gallon and the corresponding reduction in gasoline demand.

Summary

In this chapter we examined the capital stock adjustment process relating to sales of various makes and models or classes of automobiles. We found that the capital stock adjustments are critical in determining long run gasoline demand.

To summarize, we first determined that the many makes and models of cars offered in any given year may be aggregated into three classes of automobiles based on the weight and horsepower of each make and model. We used a hedonic technique to perform this aggregation and tested the stability of the relationship over time. Using the quantities generated by the hedonic equations, we in turn generated a set of demand

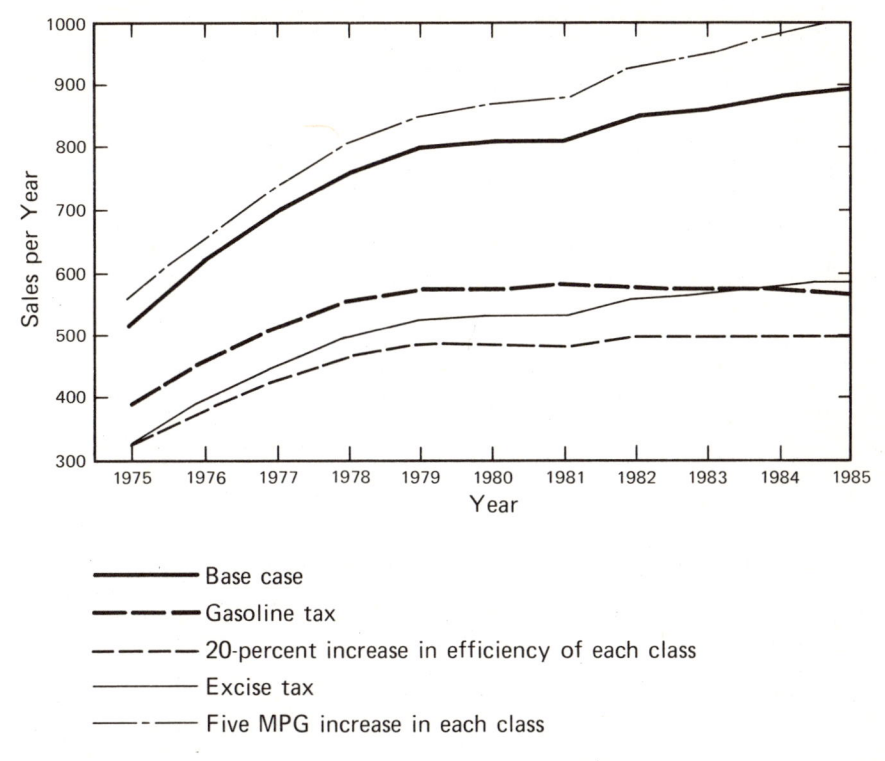

Figure 3–5. Large Car Sales—Selected Scenarios.

Legend:
—— Base case
– – – Gasoline tax
- - - - 20-percent increase in efficiency of each class
—— Excise tax
—·— Five MPG increase in each class

equations for each class of new cars. Then the demand equations were tested to determine if a commodity hierarchy existed. It was found that these unnormalized demand equations did not characterize a commodity hierarchy. Once this was determined, class demand equations were then normalized and combined with estimates of total new car sales and vehicle miles to produce estimates of gasoline demand. Then we used this model to estimate a number of elasticities, which in turn can be used to describe the effects of various policies.

We have found that policies designed to reduce gasoline demand have markedly different effects in the short run and the long run. Increases in gasoline taxes have the greatest impact in the short run, however, if the real dollar tax level is not maintained the long run, savings or demand reductions will not be as great as with other policies. Both an excise tax on large cars and an increase in technology can produce large gasoline demand reductions in the long run.

This chapter has not addressed several issues that are also important

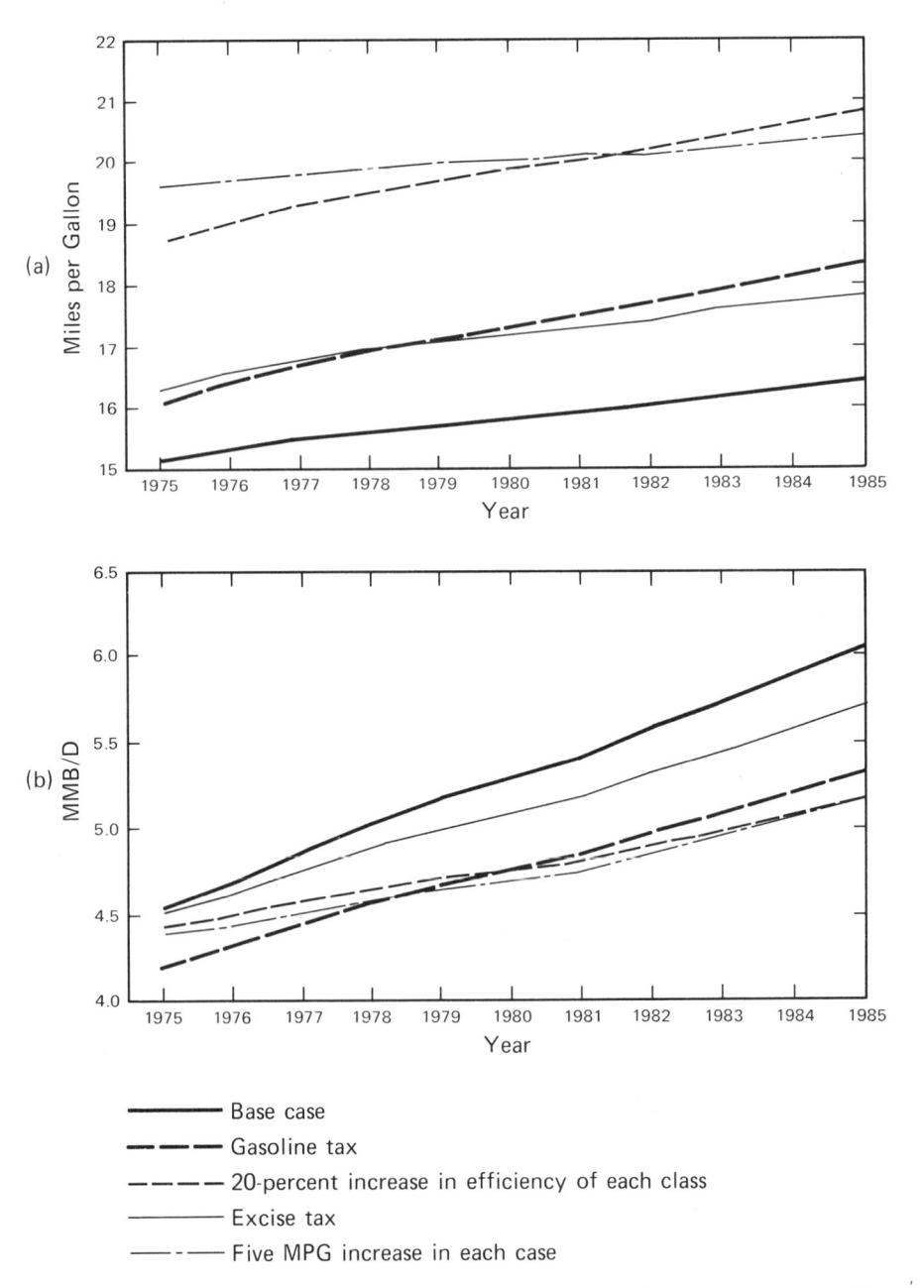

——— Base case
— — — Gasoline tax
— — — — 20-percent increase in efficiency of each class
——— Excise tax
—·—·— Five MPG increase in each case

Figure 3–6. (a) New Car Sales-Weighted MPG—Selected Scenarios; (b) Projected Gasoline Demand—Selected Scenarios.

when considering possible policies that affect gasoline demand. One issue relates to supply considerations. First, the supply function of gasoline has not been modeled, and it is very possible that an analysis including supply functions could dramatically alter the results of any policy. Second, we have implicitly assumed in this analysis that increases in technology are not accompanied by any increase in new car prices. In other words, we have not examined the marginal cost of increasing the miles per gallon of new cars. The effects of including an increasing marginal cost with respect to increasing technology also could dramatically alter the policy implications of increasing technology that have been outlined in this chapter.

Notes

1. Charlotte Chamberlin, "Policy Options: Gas Tax, U.S. Gas Rationing and/or Auto Excise Tax," Transportation System Center/WP–SP–U2–65 (Cambridge, Mass.: U.S. Department of Transportation, 1974); Philip Verleger, "A Study of the Quarterly Demand for Gasoline and Impacts of Alternative Taxes" mimeographed (Lexington, Mass.: Data Resources, Inc., 1973); J. Ramsey, A. Ramsey, A. Rasche, and B. Allen, "An Analysis of the Private and Commercial Demand for Gasoline," mimeographed (East Lansing: Michigan State University, Department of Economics, 1974); H. Houthakker and M. Kennedy, "The World Demand for Petroleum Model," mimeographed (Lexington, Mass.: Data Resources, Inc., 1974).

2. James Sweeney, "Passenger Car Use of Gasoline," working paper (Washington, D.C.: Federal Energy Administration, Office of Energy Systems, 1975); Chase Econometrics, Inc., *The Effect of Tax and Regulatory Alternatives on Car Sales and Gasoline Consumption*, submitted to the Council on Environmental Quality under contract no. EQ4AC004, January 1974; S. Wildhorn, B. Burright, J. Enns, and T. F. Kirkwood, "How to Save Gasoline: Public Policy Alternative for the Automobile," R–1560–NSF (Santa Monica, Calif.: The Rand Corporation, 1974).

3. Kelvin Lancaster, "A New Approach to Consumer Theory," *Journal of Political Economy* 74, no. 2 (April 1966): 132–157.

4. Zvi Griliches, ed., *Price Indexes and Quality Change* (Cambridge, Mass.: Harvard University Press, 1971), pp. 4–6.

5. Ibid., p. 5.

6. For a more complete discussion of commodity hierarchy theory and the associated a priori constraints, see James L. Sweeney, "Quality,

Commodity Hierarchies, and Housing Markets," *Econometrica* 42, no. 1 (January 1974): 147–165, and Derriel Cato, Mark Rodekohr, and James L. Sweeney, "Demand for Gasoline: Application of Commodity Hierarchy Theory," *Papers and Proceedings, Journal of the American Statistical Association* (Washington, D.C.: American Statistical Association, 1975): 260–264.

7. Data on population come from the U.S. Census Bureau, *Census of Population* (Washington, D.C.: U.S. Government Printing Office, various issues); data on the consumer price index come from the Bureau of Labor Statistics, *Handbook of Labor Statistics* (Washington, D.C.: U.S. Government Printing Office, various issues); and data on real disposable income come from the U.S. Department of Commerce, *National Income and Product Accounts of the U.S.* (Washington, D.C.: U.S. Government Printing Office, various issues).

8. Data on the new car miles per gallon of each class come from the U.S. Department of Transportation and U.S. Environmental Protection Agency, *Potential for Motor Vehicle Fuel Economy Improvement: Report to Congress* (Washington, D.C.: U.S. Government Printing Office, October 24, 1974). The miles per gallon data for each class were computed by observing the average weight in each class and using the corresponding miles per gallon data in the above report. Any missing data were replaced with the use of linear interpolation. Data on the price of gasoline come from the American Petroleum Institute, *Petroleum Facts and Figures* (Washington, D. C., varous issues). Sticker prices were generated by taking the simple arithmetic average of the sticker prices of all makes and models within each class. However, any imported make and model with a price of over $10,000 was eliminated from the sample.

9. See Sweeney, "Passenger Car Use of Gasoline." Mimeographed (Washington, D.C.: Federal Energy Administration, 1975).

10. See J. Kementa, *Elements of Econometrics* (New York: Macmillan, 1971), pp. 517–529, for an explanation of the seemingly unrelated regression technique.

11. See Sweeney, "Passenger Car Use of Gasoline." Mimeographed (Washington, D.C.: Federal Energy Administration, 1975).

12. Ibid.

4 Demand for Fossil Fuels by Electric Utilities

Scott E. Atkinson and Robert Halvorsen

Introduction

Approximately one-fifth of the United States' total energy consumption is in the form of electric energy produced from fossil fuels. As a result, the generation of electric energy consumes some 66 percent of coal, 8 percent of oil, and 19 percent of natural gas used for fuel and power. Thus it is necessary to analyze fossil fuel use by electric utilities to better understand both the supply of electric energy and the demand for fossil fuels.

Although there have been numerous econometric studies of the electric utility industry, little attention has been paid to the demand for individual fossil fuels. Previous studies have generally aggregated all types of fuels into a single input, and therefore they have not provided information on the elasticities of demand and substitution for each type of fuel.[a] Also, previous studies have frequently employed restrictive functional forms that imposed severe a priori constraints on the elasticities of substitution between the aggregate fuel input and other inputs.

This chapter presents estimates of all own and cross elasticities of demand and substitution for coal, oil, and natural gas. Duality theory is used to derive fuel demand equations from transcendental logarithmic profit functions. A priori restrictions on the elasticities of demand and substitution are limited to those implied by economic theory.

Estimation

The demand equations for coal, oil, and natural gas are estimated with aggregate time-series data. The equations are derived from a translog normalized restricted profit function. A classical additive disturbance term is included in each equation to reflect errors in profit-maximizing

---

Research for this chapter was supported by the Office of Energy Systems, Federal Energy Administration. We are grateful to Ernst Berndt for comments on an earlier version of this chapter and are especially grateful to David Nissen for his advice and encouragement throughout the course of our research. We retain responsibility for any remaining errors. Views expressed in the chapter are those of the authors and do not reflect in any way policies of the Federal Energy Administration.

[a]Exceptions are [10] and [12]. In [10] it is assumed that there are a limited number of discrete processes available to utilities. In [12] a branched CES production function is used to analyze interfuel substitution separately from capital and labor.

behavior. A seasonal dummy variable is included to reflect seasonal effects on fuel demands.[b]

Because cross-equation restrictions are imposed with respect to the γ_{ih}, the equations are estimated simultaneously. The off-diagonal elements of the residual covariance matrix can be expected to be nonzero, and therefore iterative Zellner-efficient estimation is used.[c] The estimates will be consistent because all explanatory variables are exogenous.

The demand equations are estimated with monthly data for August 1972 through September 1974 (26 observations); thus the total available degrees of freedom (number of observations times the number of equations) is 78.

Fuel prices are calculated from Federal Power Commission (FPC) data on expenditures and quantities purchased for each type of fuel. These prices are normalized by dividing by the price of output, calculated from FPC data on total revenue and total quantity of electric energy sold [18]. The estimated elasticities of demand and substitution indicate that substantial interfuel substitution occurs in existing plants. The estimated demand equations are used to predict demand, by month, for each type of fuel during the last quarter of 1974. The effect of gas curtailments during this period is indicated by comparing predicted demand with actual consumption.

The Model

Duality theory is used to derive systems of fuel demand equations that are consistent with profit-maximizing behavior by electric utilities. The quantity of electric energy produced is assumed to be a function of both variable and fixed inputs,

$$E = F(X;Z) \qquad (4.1)$$
$$= F(X_1, \ldots, X_m; Z_1, \ldots, Z_n), \qquad (4.2)$$

where E is electric energy, and X and Z are vectors of variable and fixed

---

[b]The seasonal dummy is equal to one for the months May through October and zero for all other months.

The effects of environmental restrictions and government oil conservation efforts on interfuel substitution are not explicitly modeled. Environmental restrictions resulted in substitution of oil for coal in some areas, while a few East Coast plants were ordered to switch from oil to coal as a result of the oil embargo. However, biases from the omission of these factors should be small because most of the substitution caused by environmental restrictions had taken place prior to the sample period, and oil-to-coal switching lasted only for a few months of the post–Arab oil embargo period.

[c]Iterative Zellner-efficient estimation is equivalent to maximum likelihood estimation of a reduced form. See [14] and [19].

inputs, respectively. Restricted profit, defined as revenue minus variable costs, is given by

$$R = bF(X;Z) - \sum_{i=1}^{m} c_i X_i, \quad (4.3)$$

where b is the price of electric energy and c_i is the price of input i.

Each utility maximizes restricted profit with respect to variable inputs given the quantities of fixed inputs, the prices of variable inputs, and the price of electric energy. The price of electric energy is determined by a regulatory agency and the prices of inputs are assumed to be determined in competitive markets. The restricted profit function, Π, is a function of b, the c_i's, and Z, which gives the maximized profit,

$$\Pi = bF(X^*_;Z) - \sum_{i=1}^{m} c_i X_i^*, \quad (4.4)$$

where the X_i^*'s are the optimized quantities of the variable inputs. Thus the restricted profit function can be written

$$\Pi = \Pi(b,c;Z) \quad (4.5)$$
$$= \Pi(b,c_1, \ldots, c_m; Z_1, \ldots Z_n). \quad (4.6)$$

A more convenient version of the restricted profit function can be obtained by noting that maximization of restricted profit is equivalent to the maximization of normalized restricted profit R^*, given by

$$R^* \equiv R/b = F(X;Z) - \sum_{i=1}^{m} P_i X_i, \quad (4.7)$$

where P_i is equal to the normalized input price, c_i/b. The corresponding normalized restricted profit function is given by

$$\Pi^* = \Pi/b = \Pi^*(\mathbf{P};Z), \quad (4.8)$$

where $\mathbf{P}$ is the vector of normalized input prices.

The principal advantage of estimating a profit function rather than a production function or cost function is that the arguments of the profit function are exogenous, so that ordinary least squares provide consistent estimates of the parameters. This advantage is not shared by production functions, whose arguments are quantities of endogenous inputs, nor by cost functions, whose arguments include the quantity of output that is endogenous.

The specification of the normalized restricted profit function used here is

$$\Pi^* = \Pi^*(P_1, P_2, P_3; Z_1, Z_2), \qquad (4.9)$$

where

P_1 = the price of coal,
P_2 = the price of oil,
P_3 = the price of gas,
Z_1 = the quantity of labor,
Z_2 = the quantity of capital,

and all prices are normalized by dividing by the price of output.

Capital is treated as a fixed input, thus avoiding the difficult task of modeling the profit-maximizing choice of capital stock. The choice of capital stock is complicated both by regulatory constraints and by peak-load demand.[d] The use of a restricted profit function permits analysis of short run profit maximizing decisions on fuel choice, given fixed capital.[e]

A number of flexible functional forms of the normalized restricted profit function could be estimated. The one used here is the transcendental logarithmic (translog):

$$\ln \Pi^* = \alpha_0 + \sum_{i=1}^{3} \alpha_i \ln P_i + \frac{1}{2} \sum_{i=1}^{3} \sum_{h=1}^{3} \gamma_{ih} \ln P_i \ln P_h$$
$$+ \sum_{i=1}^{3} \sum_{j=1}^{2} \delta_{ij} \ln P_i \ln Z_j \qquad (4.10)$$
$$+ \sum_{j=1}^{2} \beta_j \ln Z_j + \frac{1}{2} \sum_{j=1}^{2} \sum_{k=1}^{2} \phi_{jk} \ln Z_j \ln Z_k,$$

where $\gamma_{ih} = \gamma_{hi}$ and $\phi_{jk} = \phi_{kj}$. (See [5], [6], and [11].)

By Hotelling's lemma,

$$\frac{\partial \Pi^*}{\partial P_i} = -X_i^*, \qquad (4.11)$$

---

[d]It has been shown that profit maximization, subject to a rate of return constraint, results in greater use of capital than would result from cost minimization. See [2], [4], [7], and [15].

[e]These considerations are not relevant for labor inputs and it might be desirable to treat labor as a variable input. However, a labor-variable formulation produced substantially weaker results. This may have been due to the poor quality of the labor price data. Also, there is some evidence that labor is largely fixed in the short run. See [3] and [8].

where X_i^* is the profit-maximizing amount of input i. (See [9, pp. 42–45].) Using this lemma, logarithmic differentiation of the normalized restricted profit function yields demand functions for each input,

$$-\frac{\partial \ln \Pi^*}{\partial \ln P_i} = -\frac{\partial \Pi^*}{\partial P_i} \cdot \frac{P_i}{\Pi^*} = \frac{P_i X_i^*}{\Pi^*} = M_i$$

$$= -(\alpha_i + \sum_{h=1}^{3} \gamma_{ih} \ln P_h + \sum_{j=1}^{2} \delta_{ij} \ln Z_j) \qquad i = 1,2,3, \quad (4.12)$$

where M_i is the ratio of expenditures on input i to restricted profits.

The own- and cross-price elasticities of demand for fuels are readily derived from the demand functions. The own-price elasticity is defined as

$$E_{ii} = \frac{\partial X_i^*}{\partial P_i} \cdot \frac{P_i}{X_i^*}. \qquad (4.13)$$

By Hotelling's lemma,

$$X_i^* = -\frac{\partial \Pi^*}{\partial P_i}, \qquad (4.14)$$

and

$$\frac{\partial X_i^*}{\partial P_i} = -\frac{\partial^2 \Pi^*}{\partial P_i^2}. \qquad (4.15)$$

Therefore

$$E_{ii} = \frac{P_i \cdot \partial^2 \Pi^*/\partial P_i^2}{\partial \Pi^*/\partial P_i} = \frac{-M_i^2 - M_i - \gamma_{ii}}{M_i} \qquad (4.16)$$

Similarly, the cross-price elasticity is given by

$$E_{ih} = \frac{\partial X_i^*}{\partial P_h} \cdot \frac{P_h}{X_i^*} = \frac{P_h \cdot \partial^2 \Pi^*/\partial P_i \partial P_h}{\partial \Pi^*/\partial P_i} = \frac{-M_i M_h - \gamma_{ih}}{M_i}. \qquad (4.17)$$

Partial elasticities of substitution are defined as

$$\sigma_{ii} = \frac{1}{M_i} E_{ii} = \frac{-M_i^2 - M_i - \gamma_{ii}}{M_i^2} \qquad (4.18)$$

$$\sigma_{ih} = \frac{1}{M_h} E_{ih} = \frac{-M_i M_h - \gamma_{ih}}{M_i M_h}. \qquad (4.19)$$

The partial elasticities of substitution are normalized price elasticities, where the normalization is chosen such that the elasticities of substitution are invariant to the ordering of the factors. Therefore $\sigma_{ih} = \sigma_{hi}$, although in general, $E_{ih} \neq E_{hi}$.[f]

The ability of an electric utility to substitute one fuel for another will be greater in the planning stage than after the plant is in operation. In the planning stage, a utility can choose between different fuel-using technologies, but once the plant is in operation the extent of interfuel substitution is constrained by the characteristics of the capital in place. The elasticities of substitution estimated here are for existing plants. Since previous studies have frequently assumed that little or no ex post interfuel substitution can occur, it is useful to consider the mechanisms by which such substitution can take place.[g]

Interfuel substitution can occur at the plant level in two ways. First, individual generating units may be able to utilize more than one type of fuel. Second, a plant generally contains more than one generating unit, and different units may utilize different fuels. Therefore interfuel substitution can occur through changes in the merit order of individual units. Units are brought on-line in rank order according to their marginal cost of generation [16]. Changes in fuel prices alter the relative marginal cost of units using different fuels, and therefore they affect the proportion of output produced with each type of fuel.

In a previous study we used cross-section data to investigate the extent of interfuel substitution at the plant level [1]. The results indicated that significant ex post interfuel substitution does occur at the plant level. The aggregate data used in this study will also reflect opportunities for interfuel substitution beyond the plant level. For example, even if substitution were not possible at the plant level, it might occur at the firm level due to changes in the merit order of plants using different fuels. Similarly, the existence of integrated power pools makes possible further interfuel substitution through reallocations of generation requirements among firms using different fuels.

Bureau of Labor Statistics data on employment in electric companies and systems are used for labor input [17]. The quantity of capital is equal to installed generating capacity, which is measured by the manufacturer's maximum nameplate rating as reported by the FPC [18]. Normalized restricted profits are calculated as total generation from fossil fuels minus normalized expenditures on fuels.

Although the quantity of capital is not constant during the sample

---

[f]The partial elasticities defined here are analogous but not identical to Allen elasticities of substitution. They differ in two respects: Quantities rather than prices of fixed factors are held constant, and the price rather than the quantity of output is held constant.

[g]Previous studies incorporating this assumption include [8] and [13].

period, a restricted profit function remains appropriate due to the long lead times involved in changing the stock of capital. Lags in substituting between fuels should be much shorter but may still exist. The demand equations were estimated with both current fuel prices and with fuel prices lagged various numbers of months. The best results were obtained when fuel prices were lagged six months, and it is these results that are reported below.

The estimated demand equations are shown in Table 4–1. Figures in parentheses are estimated asymptotic standard errors. The value of R^2, computed as one minus the ratio of the residual sum of squares to the total sum of squares, is also shown for each equation.

Estimated elasticities of demand and substitution, evaluated at the means of the data, are shown in Table 4–2. Own elasticities should be negative and cross elasticities should be positive. Eight of the nine price elasticities have the appropriate sign, of which seven are significant at the 5-percent level. The own-price elasticity for oil has an incorrect sign but is insignificant. Five of the six elasticities of substitution have the appropriate sign, and four of these are significant. The own elasticity for oil again has an incorrect sign but is insignificant.

The cross-price elasticities are all significant and range in magnitude from 0.04 to 0.59. The magnitudes of these short run elasticities are consistent with the long run elasticities obtained with cross-section data in a previous study [1].

Table 4–1
Estimated Demand Equations

Variable		Fuel	
	Coal	Oil	Gas
Coal price	−0.220	−0.048	−0.047
	(0.049)	(0.018)	(0.043)
Oil price	−0.048	−0.217	−0.022
	(0.018)	(0.015)	(0.019)
Gas price	−0.047	−0.022	0.090
	(0.043)	(0.019)	(0.083)
Quantity of capital	−0.059	0.233	−0.039
	(0.051)	(0.110)	(0.077)
Quantity of labor	0.143	0.457	0.054
	(0.065)	(0.134)	(0.086)
Seasonal dummy	0.014	−0.002	−0.013
	(0.002)	(0.005)	(0.004)
Intercept	0.720	−4.721	0.104
	(0.867)	(1.601)	(1.055)
R^2	0.99	0.98	0.87

Table 4–2
Estimated Elasticities of Demand and Substitution[a]

	Price Elasticities of Demand[b]		Elasticities of Substitution
E_{CC}	−0.01 (0.06)	σ_{CC}	−0.03 (0.31)
E_{OO}	0.01 (0.02)	σ_{OO}	0.07 (0.19)
E_{GG}	−2.55[c] (0.12)	σ_{GG}	−42.17[c] (2.07)
E_{CG}	0.19[c] (0.01)	σ_{CG}	3.15[c] (0.18)
E_{GC}	0.59[c] (0.03)	σ_{CO}	0.98[c] (0.04)
E_{CO}	0.13[c] (0.01)	σ_{OG}	0.69[c] (0.05)
E_{OC}	0.18[c] (0.01)		
E_{OG}	0.04[c] (0.003)		
E_{GO}	0.09[c] (0.01)		

[a]Evaluated at the means of the data. Figures in parentheses are asymptotic standard errors.
[b]For cross elasticities, the quantity of the fuel indicated by the first subscript is a function of the price of the fuel indicated by the second subscript.
[c]Significant at 0.05 level.

Demand Predictions

The estimation results can be used to predict demand for coal, oil, and gas by electric utilities. From Eq. 4.12,

$$X_i^* = \frac{\Pi^*}{P_i} M_i = -\frac{\Pi^*}{P_i}\left(\alpha_i + \sum_{h=1}^{3}\gamma_{ih}\ln P_h + \sum_{j=1}^{3}\delta_{ij}\ln Z_j\right), \quad (4.20)$$

where X_i^* is the profit-maximizing quantity of fuel i, $i = C, O, G$. From Eqs. 4.4 and 4.8, predicted profit can be written,

$$\Pi^* = F(X^*;Z) - \sum_{i=1}^{3} P_i X_i^* \quad (4.21)$$

Substituting in Eq. 4.21 from Eq. 4.20,

$$\Pi^* = \frac{F(X^*;Z)}{(1 + \sum_{i=1}^{3} M_i)}. \qquad (4.22)$$

Taking output as given, and calculating the values of the M_i using the estimated parameters in Table 4–1, the value of profits can be calculated from Eq. 4.22. Substitution in Eq. 4.20 then gives the estimated demand for each type of fuel. This procedure was used to predict demand for coal, oil, and gas for October, November, and December 1974. The predicted and actual quantities are shown in Table 4–3.

Table 4–3
Predicted and Actual Fuel Consumption, 1974
(Billions of Btu's)

Fuel	October	November	December
Coal			
Predicted	739,016	761,226	798,803
Actual	768,830	774,602	844,131
Error	−29,814	−13,376	−45,328
Percent error	−3.88	−1.73	−5.37
Oil			
Predicted	244,822	240,879	249,693
Actual	256,204	271,744	300,249
Error	−11,382	−30,865	−50,556
Percent error	−4.44	−11.36	−16.84
Gas			
Predicted	341,283	302,790	285,837
Actual	309,627	247,926	213,534
Error	31,656	54,864	72,303
Percent error	10.22	22.13	33.86

Note: Error is defined as predicted minus actual.

Consumption by electric utilities of coal and oil is underestimated and consumption of gas is overestimated. The errors in predicting gas consumption are substantial, and they increase over the period considered. The overestimation of gas consumption, and the corresponding underestimation of coal and oil consumption, can be attributed to curtailments of gas supplies to electric utilities. Utilities were not able to purchase the quantities of gas desired at existing market prices due to gas rationing by suppliers. The difference between predicted and actual gas consumption provides the first available measure of the extent of gas curtailments.[h]

The results also indicate that gas curtailments affect the consumption of coal and oil about equally. For the three-month period, the total difference between predicted and actual coal consumption by electric utilities is 88,518 billion Btu's. The corresponding measure of the effect of gas curtailments on oil consumption is 92,803 billion Btu's.

Derivation of fuel demand equations from a translog profit function permits estimation of elasticities of demand and substitution that are subject only to those restrictions implied by economic theory. The estimated elasticities indicate substantial interfuel substitution in the generation of electric energy.

The finding that changes in fuel prices have significant short run effects on fossil fuel consumption has important implications for public policy. In particular, the market system appears better able to deal with exogenous shifts in energy supplies than has been frequently assumed in the formulation of public policies aimed at easing the energy crisis.

References

[1] Atkinson, Scott E. and Robert Halvorsen. "Interfuel Substitution in Steam-Electric Power Generation." Mimeographed. Washington, D.C.: Federal Energy Administration, 1975.

[2] Averch, Harvey, and Leland L. Johnson. "Behavior of the Firm under Regulatory Constraint." *American Economic Review* 52 (December 1962): 1053–1069.

[3] Barzel, Yoram. "The Production Function and Technical Change in the Steam-Power Industry." *Journal of Political Economy* 72 (April 1964): 133–150.

[4] Baumol, William J., and Alvin K. Klevorick. "Input Choices and Rate of Return Regulation: An Overview of the Discussion." *Bell Journal of Economics and Management Science* 1 (Autumn 1970): 162–190.

[5] Christensen, Laurits R., Dale W. Jorgenson, and Lawrence J. Lau. "Conjugate Duality and the Transcendental Logarithmic Production Function." *Econometrica* 39 (July 1971): 255–256.

[6] ———. "Transcendental Logarithmic Production Frontiers." *Review of Economics and Statistics* 55 (February 1973): 28–45.

---

[h]Estimates of gas curtailments are published by the Federal Power Commission for interstate but not intrastate gas sales. Intrastate sales account for about one-half of total gas consumption by electric utilities.

[7] Courville, Leon. "Regulation and Efficiency in the Electric Utility Industry." *Bell Journal of Economics and Management Science* 5 (Spring 1974): 53–74.

[8] Dhrymes, Phoebus J., and Mordecai Kurz. "Technology and Scale in Electricity Generation." *Econometrica* 32 (July 1964): 287–315.

[9] Diewert, W. E. "Applications of Duality Theory." In M. Intrilligator and D. Kendrick (eds.), *Frontiers in Quantitative Economics,* vol. 2. Amsterdam: North-Holland Publishing Company, 1974.

[10] Joskow, Paul L., and Frederic S. Mishkin. "Electric Utility Fuel Choice Behavior in the United States." Mimeographed. Washington, D.C.: Public Utility Board, 1974.

[11] Lau, Lawrence J. "Some Applications of Profit Functions." Research Center in Economic Growth Memoranda no. 86A and 86B. Stanford, Calif.: Stanford University, November 1969.

[12] Lawrence, Anthony G. "Inter-fuel Substitution: Steam Electric Generation's Demand for Fuels." Research Division, Office of Prices and Living Conditions, Discussion Paper no. 8. Washington, D.C.: U.S. Bureau of Labor Statistics, 1972.

[13] McFadden, Daniel. "Notes on the Estimation of the Elasticity of Substitution." Institute of Business and Economic Research, Working Paper no. 57. Berkeley: University of California, December 1964.

[14] Oberhofer, W., and J. Kmenta. "A General Procedure for Obtaining Maximum Likelihood Estimates in Generalized Regression Models." *Econometrica* 42 (May 1974): 579–590.

[15] Spann, Robert M. "Rate of Return Regulation and Efficiency in Production: An Empirical Test of the Averch-Johnson Thesis." *Bell Journal of Economics and Management Science* 5 (Spring 1974): 38–52.

[16] Turvey, Ralph. *Optimal Pricing and Investment in Electricity Supply.* Cambridge, Mass.: The M.I.T. Press, 1968.

[17] U.S. Bureau of Labor Statistics. *Employment and Earnings.* Washington, D.C.: U.S. Department of Labor, various months.

[18] U.S. Federal Power Commission, *Monthly Forms* 4, 5, and 453. Washington, D.C.: U.S. Federal Power Commission, various months.

[19] Zellner, Arnold. "An Efficient Method of Estimating Seemingly Unrelated Regressions and Tests for Aggregation Bias." *Journal of the American Statistical Association* 57 (June 1962): 348–368.

5

An Application of Spatial Equilibrium Analysis to Electrical Energy Allocation

Noel D. Uri

Introduction

Recently, discussion concerning the regional coordination of the generation, pricing, and allocation of electrical energy in the United States has increased. For instance, an industry committee advising the Federal Power Commission on matters affecting reliability stressed that regional coordination was the most effective and economical method of achieving desired reliability standards [3, p. 27]. The rationale underlying the suggestion is based on economic and social concerns.

A society's financial and environmental structure both benefit from transmission ties: Regional coordination, or "pooling," in general offers distinct economies to participating systems and environmental savings to society. Because of time-of-day diversities (and the noncoincidental occurrence of demand peaks of participating systems) it is possible to reduce the total electrical energy capacity requirement that otherwise would apply if each system acted independently.

Specifically, the financial structure of a system is altered in several ways through broad-based economy dispatch. The primary change is the operational cost savings. In addition, electrical energy peak capacity and reserve requirements are reduced. Economies of scale are realized through pooling. But with capacity costs increasing and utility interest coverage ratios approaching minimum trust indenture specification, it will be difficult for even the larger systems to finance unilaterally the extensive capacity installations projected for the next 20 years.

In addition to economic advantages, regional coordination offers the social advantage of maximizing environmental efficiencies. Duplication of generation or transmission facilities results in a misallocation of resources. Maximum use of each site, multiple use of existing transmission rights-of-way, and their conversion into interutility transmission corridors are possible. Such conversion increases both economic and environmental efficiency. Pooling seems to provide economic and social cost minimization options to the largest utility systems while simultaneously extending those benefits to an additional segment of the industry.

This chapter focuses on economic options. Specifically, I examine what impact would be realized by changing to a completely integrated system of generating and distributing electrical energy from the present situation of little or no interutility coordination. In a completely integrated system, market forces operate in an uninhibited way to determine prices of electrical energy.

The Model

For our analysis let us look at various regions with a multiconsuming sector that operates under a market economy for electrical energy. The analysis assumes that known linear functions relate the quantity produced and consumed to the price of electrical energy to each consuming sector in each region and where the regions are separated by known transmission costs. The objective of designing the analysis in this way is to set out a spatial equilibrium model that converts the problem of spatial pricing and allocation to an extremum problem with the objective of maximizing net social payoff. We define net social payoff, in terms of the underlying demand and supply relations for all regions, as the areas under the regional excess demand function minus the total transmission and distribution costs.

Before examining the model, it is convenient to introduce the requisite definitions and notation. Let

- i where $i = 1, 2, \ldots, L$ denote the consuming sectors,
- j, k where $j, k = 1, 2, \ldots, M$ denote the regions,
- θ where $\theta = 1, 2, \ldots, N$ denote the plant type for generating electrical energy,
- y_{ij} denote the quantity of electrical energy demanded by the ith consuming sector in the jth region,
- x_{jk} denote the quantity of electrical energy transmitted interregionally (where $j \neq k$) and distributed intraregionally (where $j = k$),
- x_j^θ denote the net quantity of electrical energy generated in region j by plant type θ,
- K_j^θ denote the net generating capacity of plant type θ existing in region j,
- d_{jk} denote the distribution cost of electrical energy generated in region j and distributed in region k,
- t_{jk} denote the transmission cost of electrical energy from region j to region k,
- α_j^θ denote the marginal operation and maintenance cost (including fuel cost) for a plant of type θ, and
- β_j^θ denote the marginal cost per unit capacity (capital cost) for plant type θ in region j.

Based on the assumption that linear demand functions of each consumer are known with certainty or are available in the certainty equivalence sense, the demand functions are given in the following form:

$$p_{ij} = a_{ij} - b_{ij} y_{ij}, \tag{5.1}$$

where p_{ij} is the price of electrical energy to consumer i in region j, and $a_{ij} > 0$ and $b_{ij} \geq 0$ for all i and j.

The price of generating electrical energy consists not only of operating and maintenance costs but also of the capital cost incurred when the generating plant was constructed. Thus the supply price is assumed to be a function of these costs whereby

$$p_j^\theta = \alpha_j^\theta + \beta_j^\theta, \tag{5.2}$$

where p_j^θ is the supply price of electrical energy in region j by plant type θ.

To determine optimum demands, prices, and operating schedules we need to restrict our model by the following constraints:

1. For each region the total quantity of electrical energy demanded must be less than or equal to the quantity supplied by that region plus the quantity transmitted from other regions, that is,

$$\sum_i y_{ik} \leq \sum_j x_{jk} \quad \text{for all } i, j, \text{ and } k. \tag{5.3}$$

2. For each region the total net transmission and distribution of electrical energy is less than or equal to the net generation from all plants within that region, stated as

$$\sum_k x_{jk} \leq \sum_\theta x_j^\theta \quad \text{for all } i, j, k, \text{ and } \theta. \tag{5.4}$$

3. For each type of plant in each region, net generation is less than or equal to the net generating capacity available for that plant type, given by

$$x_j^\theta \leq K_j^\theta \quad \text{for all } j \text{ and } \theta. \tag{5.5}$$

A Spatial Equilibrium Model

Given the definitions and constraints outlined in the previous section it is now possible to display the total net quasi-welfare function W for the spatial equilibrium model:[a]

---

[a] See Hotelling [6] for the rationale underlying this formulation.

$$W(x,y) = \sum_i \sum_j \int (a_{ij} - b_{ij}y_{ij})dy_{ij}$$
$$- \sum_j \sum_\theta \alpha_j^\theta x_j^\theta - \sum_j \sum_\theta \beta_j^\theta x_j^\theta \qquad (5.6)$$
$$- \sum_j \sum_k d_{jk}x_{jk} - \sum_j \sum_k t_{jk}x_{jk}.$$

If the demand curves are downward sloping ($b_{ij} \geq 0$), then the net quasi-welfare function is concave. The necessary conditions for the maximum of this function can be obtained by rewriting the problem in the Lagrangian form

$$\phi(x,y,\lambda) = W(x,y) + \lambda'\Omega(x,y),$$

where $\Omega(x,y)$ is the constraint set. Specifically, associate the dual variables λ_{1j}, λ_{2j}, and $\lambda_{\theta j}$ with constraints (5.3) through (5.5), respectively. These dual variables are defined below. The relations displayed in (5.7) through (5.12) present the necessary conditions for an optimum.

$(a_{ij} - b_{ij}y_{ij}) - \lambda_{1j} \leq 0$	$y_{ij} \leq 0.$	(5.7)
$-d_{jk} - t_{jk} + \lambda_{1k} - \lambda_{2j} \leq 0$	$x_{jk} \leq 0.$	(5.8)
$-\alpha_j - \beta_j^\theta + \lambda_{2j} - \lambda_{\theta j} \leq 0$	$x_j^\theta \leq 0.$	(5.9)
$\sum_j x_{jk} - \sum_i y_{ik} \geq 0$	$\lambda_{1k} \geq 0.$	(5.10)
$\sum_\theta x_j^\theta - \sum_k x_{jk} \geq 0$	$\lambda_{2j} \geq 0.$	(5.11)
$K_j^\theta - x_j^\theta \geq 0$	$\lambda_{\theta j} \geq 0.$	(5.12)

Condition (5.7) states that when demand is positive, the demand price in a given region λ_{1j} must be exactly equal to the market demand price p_{ij} prevailing across all consuming sectors in a region. Thus if

$$y_{ij} > 0,$$

then

$$a_{ij} - b_{ij}y_{ij} = p_{ij}. \qquad (5.7a)$$

If demand is zero, then the demand price λ_{ij} is either less than or equal to the market demand price p_{ij} for each consuming sector in a region. Thus if

$$y_{ij} = 0,$$

then

$$p_{ij} \leq \lambda_{1j}. \tag{5.7b}$$

Condition (5.8) states that when the optimal transmission and distribution of electrical energy is positive, the difference between the market demand and market supply prices, λ_{1k}, λ_{2j}, is equal to the interregional transmission cost plus intraregional distribution cost. Thus if

$$x_{jk} > 0,$$

then

$$\lambda_{1k} - \lambda_{2j} = d_{jk} + t_{jk}. \tag{5.8a}$$

If the optimal transmission and distribution is zero, the difference is less than or equal to the sum of these two costs. Thus if

$$x_{jk} = 0,$$

then

$$\lambda_{1k} - \lambda_{2j} \leq d_{jk} + t_{jk}. \tag{5.8b}$$

$\lambda_{\theta j}$ may be interpreted as the quasi rent of plant type θ in region j. Consequently, condition (5.9) states that when there is a positive net generation on plant type θ, the quasi rent is equal to the difference between the supply price and the operating cost. Thus if

$$x_j^\theta > 0,$$

then

$$\lambda_{\theta j} = \lambda_{2j} - \alpha_j^\theta - \beta_j^\theta. \tag{5.9a}$$

If the optimal generation using plant type θ is zero, the quasi rent is less than or equal to the difference between the supply price and the generating cost plus capital cost. Thus if

$$x_j^\theta = 0,$$

then

$$\lambda_{\theta j} \leq \lambda_{2j} \, \alpha_j^\theta - \beta_j^\theta. \tag{5.9b}$$

To minimize total cost, production will be scheduled on equipment in increasing order of operating cost plus capital cost so that supply price in any region equals the operating plus capital costs on the least efficient, or "marginal," plant type then in use in that region. Thus denoting the least efficient plant type by θ^* and if

$$0 < x_j^{\theta*} < K^{\theta*},$$

then

$$\lambda_{2j} = \alpha_j^{\theta*} + \beta_j^\theta. \tag{5.13}$$

The quasi rent of any plant type in use is, in fact, the difference between its operating and capital costs and those costs of the marginal plant. Thus if

$$x_j^\theta > 0,$$

then

$$\lambda_{\theta j} = (\alpha_j^{\theta*} + \beta_j^{\theta*}) - (\alpha_j^\theta + \beta_j^\theta). \tag{5.14}$$

Model Parameter Estimates

Before presenting our results it is necessary to describe the economic setting. Specifically, the various regions, classes of consumers, plant types, and other features of regions examined are clearly defined. The regional classification used in our analysis is the Bureau of the Census's nine-region division of the contiguous United States.[b] Within each region three consuming sectors are considered: residential, commercial, and

---

[b]The Regional Classification is as follows:

1. New England (Maine, New Hampshire, Vermont, Massachusetts, Rhode Island, Connecticut)
2. Middle Atlantic (New York, New Jersey, Pennsylvania)
3. East North Central (Ohio, Indiana, Illinois, Michigan, Wisconsin)
4. West North Central (Minnesota, Iowa, Missouri, North Dakota, South Dakota, Nebraska, Kansas)
5. South Atlantic (Delaware, Maryland and D.C., Virginia, West Virginia, North Carolina, South Carolina, Georgia, Florida)
6. East South Central (Kentucky, Tennessee, Alabama, Mississippi)
7. West South Central (Arkansas, Louisiana, Oklahoma, Texas)
8. Mountain (Montana, Idaho, Wyoming, Colorado, New Mexico, Arizona, Utah, Nevada)
9. Pacific (Washington, Oregon, California).

industrial. There is a fourth sector, nominally called "other," that consists of agricultural consumption, transportation consumption, governmental consumption, and interdepartmental consumption. This sector accounted for 3.8 percent of total electrical energy consumed in 1973. But because of this sector's heterogeneous composition and its overall unresponsiveness to price changes, it is assumed that this sector can purchase any desired quantity of electricity at the prevailing market price, and hence that it will be omitted from explicit consideration.

On the supply side, three alternative methods of generating electrical energy are considered: hydroelectric plants, fossil-fueled steam-electrical plants (coal, oil, and gas), and nuclear steam plants. Internal combustion, a fourth method of generating electrical energy, is not included because it accounted for only 0.33 percent of total generation in 1973. To implement the model empirically it is necessary to know the demand and supply functions in linear price-dependent relations. When estimating the demand curves for electrical energy, various econometric problems develop [7, Chapter 2]. Consequently, the demand curves are obtained by first estimating the price elasticity for each region and consumer sector. A variable elasticity model is specified for each consuming sector where the quantity of electrical energy consumed in a region in any year is assumed to be a function of the quantity of electrical energy consumed in the previous year, the average price of electrical energy for that year, the per capita personal income for that year, and the price of natural gas in the previous year. The price elasticities are estimated upon pooling cross-section and time-series data for each consuming sector across all regions for the time period from 1946 to 1973. Regionally, the price elasticities range between -0.154 and -0.160 for the residential sector, between -0.0279 and -0.282 for the commercial sector, and between -0.22 and -0.184 for the industrial sector. Using these elasticities, the actual quantity demanded, and actual price of electrical energy in 1973, we obtain the estimate of the linear demand functions [7, p. 34].

For the supply side, operating costs are obtained from the Federal Power Commission. Average annual production expenses (which are assumed equal to marginal operating cost) for the various plant types are estimated for 1973 for a representative selection of plants in each region from Forms no. 1 and 1–M filed with the Federal Power Commission. To estimate the capital cost of the various plant types, a technique developed at Oak Ridge National Laboratory was used because the actual values were not available [1]. The technique takes into account intraregional variation in land, structure, and equipment as well as vintage considerations—that is, different ages of generating capacity. A detailed discussion of the technique is discussed by Uri [7, pp. 56–59]. Capital cost estimates for hydroelectric plants vary between $215 and $250 per kilowatt; for fossil-fueled steam-electric plants they range between $269 and $398; and for nuclear plants they range between $303 and $364 per kilowatt. Given these capital cost estimates, per unit (kilowatt-hour) cost is calculated based on a number of independent variables: (1) the service life of a particular plant type; (2) the total net generation expected each year; (3) the rate of equipment depreciation; (4) the annual rate of fixed charges—the cost of money, interim replacements, insurance, and taxes; and (5) a rate-of-return on investment.

Interregional transmission cost per kilowatt-hour per mile is computed from data supplied by the Federal Power Commission. It is determined that the marginal cost of transmitting one kilowatt-hour of electrical energy one mile is 0.00478 mills.[c] Nine demand points are used in the model for the purpose of measuring the distance between region j and region k. The resulting distance times the marginal cost of transmission will produce the cost of transmitting one kilowatt-hour between region j and region k. The demand areas are large and it is difficult to select a single location as representative of an entire region. The method used to select a representative location is to weigh each set of coordinates in a region by the consumption of electrical energy at that location, the average distance traveled by each kilowatt-hour through a region, and the maximum distance that electrical energy would have to travel.

Intraregional distribution cost is obtained from the *1970 National Power Survey* [4] (inflated to account for price increases) and represents an average for all electric utilities in the contiguous United States. No attempt has been made to break the cost down by region, type of ownership, or any other system of classification. Given the relatively low level of spatial resolution, regional averages will closely approximate the national average, and hence this value can be used without severe reservations. The figure used is 6.05 mills per kilowatt-hour.

Finally, the net generating capacity is obtained from the *Statistical Year Book of the Electric Utility Industry for 1973* [2] and reflects the actual net generation in 1973.

As a final comment before turning to a solution of the model, note that all values of the primal variables in the problem formulation are given in net terms.

The Spatial Equilibrium Solution

This investigation seeks to develop a policy that will insure that net social payoff (social welfare) is maximized relative to available electrical energy

---

[c]Uri [8] explains the derivation of this estimate for 1970. This value is then inflated to 1973 prices.

supply. Economic theory indicates that such a situation is approached when a competitive market prevails. Under this condition, the market price of electrical energy should equal the marginal cost of supplying electrical energy to the market, which in turn is equal to the value in use of the last kilowatt-hour purchased by consumers. This is exactly what the Kuhn-Tucker conditions for optimality guarantee. The model indicates that when regional coordination operates, the total value of the net social payoff is $123,786 million.

Assuming that a competitive market prevails across all consumer sectors, plant types, and regions, the solution to the spatial equilibrium model can be found. The results are presented in Tables 5–1 through 5–5. The supply prices are not given, but they can be computed quickly by subtracting the distribution cost and transmission cost, if any, from the demand.

The optimal quantities demanded by each sector for each one of the regions changes from the actual amount consumed in 1973, as one would expect given that a uniform price is charged to each consuming sector in a region. The optimal quantity demanded by the residential sector increases

Table 5–1
Equilibrium Demand for Electrical Energy by Sector and Region, 1973
(per kWh in billions)

Region	Residential	Commercial	Industrial
New England (NE)	27.15 (27.37)	20.38 (20.70)	20.09 (20.43)
Middle Atlantic (MA)	73.47 (73.47)	64.48 (64.48)	83.95 (83.95)
East North Central (ENC)	99.44 (100.85)	69.54 (71.35)	146.63 (150.18)
West North Central (WNC)	43.95 (44.75)	27.74 (28.69)	35.66 (36.79)
South Atlantic (SA)	108.42 (111.41)	70.20 (73.66)	88.38 (91.76)
East South Central (ESC)	50.51 (52.99)	20.23 (21.87)	89.85 (91.46)
West South Central (WSC)	64.57 (64.82)	47.11 (47.48)	76.95 (77.18)
Mountain (M)	24.51 (24.53)	25.69 (25.73)	25.14 (25.16)
Pacific (P)	76.43 (76.43)	68.03 (68.03)	83.39 (83.39)

Note: The values when transmission is restricted are in parentheses.

Table 5-2
Equilibrium Flows of Electrical Energy Generated in 1973
(by region, kWh in billions)

	New England	Middle Atlantic	East North Central	West North Central	South Atlantic	East South Central	West South Central	Mountain	Pacific
NE[a]	67.62 (68.50)	2.43 (0.0)							
MA		98.46 (221.89)							
ENC		15.30 (0.0)	315.61 (322.39)						
WNC		18.94 (0.0)		91.30 (110.23)					
SA		52.18 (0.0)			267.00 (276.83)				
ESC		15.98 (0.0)				161.00 (166.32)			
WSC		18.61 (0.0)					188.63 (189.47)		
M				16.06 (0.0)				75.35 (75.42)	
P									227.85 (227.85)

Note: The values when transmission is restricted are in parentheses.

[a]The regional abbreviations denote the New England Region, the Middle Atlantic Region, and so on.

Table 5-3
Equilibrium Generation by Plant Type and Region, 1973
(per kWh in billions)

	Plants		
Region	Hydro-electric	Fossil	Nuclear
New England	5.22	50.82	14.01
	(5.22)	(49.28)	(14.01)
Middle Atlantic	28.71	59.13	10.62
	(28.70)	(182.56)	(10.62)
East North Central	3.71	299.41	27.79
	(3.71)	(290.88)	(27.79)
West North Central	11.93	94.56	3.74
	(11.93)	(94.56)	(3.74)
South Atlantic	18.64	283.45	17.08
	(18.64)	(241.11)	(17.08)
East South Atlantic	26.61	149.70	0.27
	(26.61)	(139.71)	(0.27)
West South Central	9.39	197.85	0.0
	(9.39)	(189.47)	(0.0)
Mountain	26.67	64.73	0.0
	(26.67)	(48.75)	(0.0)
Pacific	128.11	93.03	6.71
	(128.11)	(93.03)	(6.71)

Note: The values when transmission is restricted are in parentheses.

on the average by about 5 percent over actual consumption in 1973, and the optimal quantity demanded by the commercial sector is about 6 percent larger on the average than actual consumption. For the industrial sector, optimal quantity demanded falls by about 5 percent from actual 1973 consumption. Thus in 1973 not only were the residential and commercial sectors charged too high a price on the average, they were also allocated less than what would have been optimal from a social welfare perspective.

Marginal cost pricing underlies the model to determine the optimal pricing profile. In the model, the full marginal cost is charged. This consists of marginal operating cost, distribution cost, capital cost, plus any transmission cost if electrical energy is transmitted into the region. In addition, a quasi rent accrues to the utilities because of the fixed generating capacity. On the basis of the marginal cost criterion, the regulatory commissions are remiss in setting the rate structure in some regions. With the exception of the East South Central region, West South Central region, and Pacific region, the average price paid in 1973 is too high by 5

Table 5–4
Equilibrium Demand Price by Region, 1973
(mills per kWh)

Region	Price
New England	23.10
	(21.45)
Middle Atlantic	24.13
	(24.13)
East North Central	20.11
	(17.69)
West North Central	18.35
	(15.27)
South Atlantic	20.01
	(16.05)
East South Central	19.45
	(14.53)
West South Central	16.46
	(15.91)
Mountain	15.45
	(15.34)
Pacific	16.72
	(16.72)

Note: The price when transmission is restricted is given in parentheses.

to 13 percent. In the other regions, the average price is approximately equal to the competitive norm.

A most revealing aspect of the results is the significant interregional transmissions that would have been desirable from the viewpoint of social welfare maximization in 1973. The greatest transmission of electrical energy is into the Middle Atlantic region. Because of the cost differentials—especially the high operating cost in the Middle Atlantic region for fossil-fuel steam-electric plants relative to the generating costs in the other regions—it would have been optimal to let consumers in other regions bear some of the burden of the high cost of fuel, principally oil, in the Middle Atlantic region. In fact, more than one-half of the electrical energy consumed in that region should have come from other regions.

Restriction on Transmission

It is remarkable how little electrical energy appears currently to be transmitted from state to state or from region to region. With the expansion of the extra high voltage lines, increased interconnection of power systems

Table 5-5
Quasi Rent of a Particular Plant Type, 1973
(mills per kWh)

	Plants		
Region	Hydro-electric	Fossil	Nuclear
New England	10.50 (8.86)	1.65 (0.0)	8.39 (6.75)
Middle Atlantic	11.98 (11.98)	0.0 (0.0)	6.79 (6.79)
East North Central	8.42 (6.00)	2.43 (0.0)	7.17 (4.74)
West North Central	5.50 (2.42)	3.10 (0.02)	4.85 (1.78)
South Atlantic	8.00 (4.04)	3.96 (0.0)	6.85 (2.89)
East South Central	8.69 (3.78)	4.91 (0.0)	4.76 (0.0)
West South Central	0.37 (0.0)	0.54 (0.0)	4.80 (4.26)
Mountain	2.62 (2.51)	0.11 (0.0)	4.82 (4.71)
Pacific	5.09 (5.09)	1.35 (1.35)	2.11 (2.11)

Note: The values when transmission is restricted are in parentheses.

makes it feasible to transmit electrical energy over long distances. Unfortunately, this is not yet an accepted part of the electrical energy picture [5]. This section presents evidence that the lack of interregional energy transmission has a negative effect on social welfare, i.e., consumers in the aggregate are worse off.

What would be the quantitative impact on society of restricting interregional transmission of electrical energy if the electric utility industry were to operate in a perfectly competitive environment? By imposing the constraint $x_{jk} = 0$ for $j \neq k$ and all j and k, it is possible to answer this question.

Associating the dual variable λ_{3jk} with this constraint and with the other dual variables defined as above, the Kuhn-Tucker conditions will remain unchanged with one exception and one addition. The exception is that condition (5.8) becomes

$$-d_{jk} - t_{jk} + \lambda_{1k} - \lambda_{2j} - \lambda_{3jk} \leq 0 \qquad x_{jk} \geq 0. \qquad (5.8c)$$

The addition is condition (5.15) where

$$x_{jk} \leq 0 \qquad \lambda_{3jk} \geq 0. \qquad (5.15)$$

Condition (5.8c) states that when the optimal transmission and distribution of electrical energy is positive, the difference between the market demand and market supply prices is equal to the interregional transmission cost plus distribution cost plus a penalty arising because of the restriction of interregional flows. Thus in the region into which electrical energy would have been optimally transmitted, the utility will receive a quasi rent equal to the transmission cost plus the penalty, λ_{3jk}.

The results of imposing the transmission restriction are found in Tables 5-1 through Table 5-6. Of particular interest are the quasi rents on transmission restrictions. One can see that the quasi rents are greater than the transmission costs in the regions where transmission occurred in the unrestricted model, but in several other situations, a penalty due to the constraint is incurred with a resultant higher price though it does not indicate that the consumer in a region has a strong enough desire to have additional electrical energy.

The total value of the net social payoff when transmission is restricted is equal to $123,487 million. Both the primal and dual variables behave as predicted. Regions that have an economic advantage in the generation of electrical energy are able to supply a greater quantity at a lower price to their customers. This is at the expense of other regions that are forced to charge a higher price with a resultant decrease in the quantity demanded. In the former case, regional social payoff expands, and in the latter, regional social payoff contracts. In the aggregate, society is worse off.

Table 5-6
Quasi Rent on Transmission Restriction, 1973
(mills per kWh)

Region From	Region To	Quasi Rent
New England	Middle Atlantic	1.65
East North Central	Middle Atlantic	2.43
West North Central	Middle Atlantic	3.08
West North Central	East North Central	0.01
South Atlantic	New England	0.27
South Atlantic	Middle Atlantic	3.96
East South Central	New England	1.23
East South Central	Middle Atlantic	4.92
East South Central	East North Central	0.04
East South Central	South Atlantic	0.78
West South Central	Middle Atlantic	0.54

Sensitivity of the Results

Although the model yields some interesting conclusions, the interpretations would be misleading if the results depended on the specific paramters used. The estimates of costs are by no means perfectly accurate. If slight changes in the estimates lead to major changes in conclusions, then the model is not at all interesting.

The effects on pricing and allocation for each region could be determined by incrementally changing all the cost components. This would require an elaborate procedure. In light of the optimality conditions, however, it is not necessary to go through such a laborious process. By looking at the Kuhn-Tucker conditions, one can see, for positive quantities of the primal variables, what regional differentials are needed to induce interregional transmission.

The one estimate crucial to the empirical implementation of the model whose influence on the results is not immediately clear is the estimate of the price elasticity. For example, it is well known that omitting variables when specifying a demand equation will bias the estimates of ordinary least squares. It should be apparent that some important variables have not been included in the demand equations used to estimate the price elasticities. Consequently, the model was solved both with and without transmission restriction where it is assumed that the true price elasticity is only one-half as well as twice the estimated value.

For the situation when one-half the elasticity estimate is used for each of the consumer sectors across all regions, there is a slight decline in the quantity of electrical energy demanded amounting to 15 percent or less depending on the consumer sector and region. The price of electrical energy, because of the structure of the operating cost, capital cost, distribution cost, and transmission cost, does not change in any of the regions. Interregional transmission remains intact at about the same order of magnitude. The value of the net social payoff is slightly less than twice the value when the original elasticity is used. When interregional transmissions are restricted and one-half the estimated value of the price elasticity is used, the results, relative to no transmission restrictions, are analogous to the results presented in the restriction on transmission section. Similarly, when twice the elasticity estimates are used, there are small, though insignificant, changes in the results.

Summary

In the introduction to this chapter we asked what would be the impact of moving to a fully integrated network for the electrical energy industry in the United States. The model that was developed has attempted to answer this question. The results are not meant to indicate that there is only one way to alter the structure of the electrical energy industry, but rather to indicate directions that current discussions should move.

First, a misallocation of electrical energy among consuming sectors in each region currently exists. Because the price of electrical energy is too high for the residential and commercial sectors and too low for the industrial sector, the industrial sector consumes a greater quantity of electrical energy than what the social optimum would allow at the expense of the residential and commercial sectors. Second, the welfare of society could be enhanced if the industry operation were carried out by the utilities on a national basis where it would be possible for all regions to benefit from the economic advantages that a few possess in the generation of electrical energy. Finally, the electrical energy industry on the average does not adhere to a marginal cost-pricing rule. Marginal cost pricing means paying for assets when they are being used, not before they are acquired. It is evident from the empirical results that the industry is charging a price that exceeds the marginal cost of supplying electrical energy.

References

[1] Bowers, H.I., *CONCEPT—Computerized Conceptual Cost Estimates of Steam Electric Power Plants*, ORNL-4809. Oak Ridge, Tenn. Oak Ridge National Laboratory, 1973.

[2] Edison Electric Institute. *Statistical Year Book of the Electric Utility Industry, 1973*. New York: Edison Electric Institute, 1974.

[3] Federal Power Commission. *Prevention of Power Failure*, vol. II. Washington, D.C.: Federal Power Commission, 1967.

[4] ———. *1970 National Power Survey*. Washington, D.C.: Federal Power Commission, 1971.

[5] Hall, F. P., and G. N. Broderick. *Supply and Demand for Energy in the United States*, Information Circular 8402. Washington, D.C.: Government Printing Office. 1969.

[6] Hotelling, H. "Edgeworth Taxation Paradox and the Nature of Demand and Supply Functions." *Journal of Political Economy* 40 (1932): 577–616.

[7] Uri, Noel D. *Towards an Efficient Allocation of Electrical Energy*. Lexington, Mass.: Lexington Books, D. C. Heath and Company, 1975.

[8] Uri, Noel D. "A Note on the Cost of Transmitting Electrical Energy." *Nebraska Journal of Economics and Business* 15, No. 1 (Winter 1975): 55–60.

6

Short Term Forecasts of Energy Supply and Demand

Christopher Alt, Anthony Bopp, and George Lady

Introduction

This chapter presents eight petroleum forecasting equations used on a day-to-day basis to provide quantitative economic analysis for energy policy-makers. The equations presented in this chapter were developed in support of policy analysis to forecast the monthly demand for eight petroleum product categories. Three major policy issues were explored: (1) fuel sufficiency, given regulated prices, over the range of plausible expectations about future economic activity and weather variations (e.g., will there be enough fuel oil if next winter is especially cold?); (2) the alternative petroleum demand rates associated with alternative policy options for the decontrol (or not) of oil prices (e.g., how much lower will oil imports be next year if we decontrol now or if we do nothing?); and (3) a retrospective assessment of the degree to which various economic propositions appear to have been actually realized (e.g., do higher prices really result in lower consumption in the short run?).

In one variation or another such issues could arise frequently with an associated requirement for immediate resolution. A consideration of the class of policy analysis issues to be supported is necessary to understand the evaluation of the petroleum forecasting equations. While forecasts must be "accurate," the forecasting methods must also incorporate the factors and influences that are the dimensions of the policy-makers' concern. Generally, a policy debate will concern many alternative "futures" and their ramifications, while at most only one such "future" can be realized. Accordingly, a policy analysis tool must distinguish among the alternatives at issue if it is to be useful in the policy analysis process. The general structure and specification of the forecasting equations presented here were chosen not only on the basis of predictive criteria, but on the basis of the policy analysis problems to be addressed.

To support the three policy problem areas noted, the petroleum demand equations must generally account for the effects of the level of economic activity, relative energy prices, the intertemporal structure of such relationships, and the weather. Despite the very large number of alternative specifications that were attempted, we found that significant inference for all four relationships could not be achieved simultaneously. The forecasting procedures documented here were chosen to accommodate the policy requirement that all these influences be accounted for one way or the other.

Equation Specifications

The eight petroleum consumption equations presented in this chapter satisfy the foregoing criteria. They have provided accurate forecasts of petroleum product consumption, and they were used repeatedly in the national debate about decontrolling the price of oil. The equations are useful because they (1) separate and identify variations in consumption due to weather from changes due to economic factors; (2) demonstrate statistically significant price effects, if any price variables were included; (3) accommodate changes in macroeconomic variables in a significant manner; and (4) relate to longer term models in a consistent manner. Only if one understands these four requirements can one understand the final functional forms used to forecast petroleum consumption.

The separation of weather effects from economic effects was important for three reasons. First, if any price effects were to be included, historical variations in consumption due to weather variation needed to be distinguished from those due to higher prices. If not, biased estimation of price effects would have resulted and policy alternatives based on higher prices would have lacked supporting analysis. Second, cold weather scenarios were generally of interest. Forecasts that revealed no heating oil "shortages" at current prices were forced to consider a cold weather scenario as a real alternative to the normal weather case. Finally, various conservation scenarios often included fuel conservation measures that resulted from voluntary consumer action in choosing lower heat levels for their homes and businesses. If one can forecast weather effects, one can also estimate the effects of such conservation measures.

The second requirement often imposed on short term energy forecasts is that included price effects be significant. A substantial body of literature demonstrates long term energy price effects, but there is also substantial skepticism concerning the ability of prices to affect energy consumption levels significantly in the short run. For the petroleum forecasting equations presented here, all the major products and almost all the other products have significant price terms. In two instances, a specification revealing significant price effects could not be found.

It has been stated in the econometric literature that statistically insignificant variables should not be omitted, especially if the coefficient is large. Satisfactory definitions of "largeness" are not found in the literature. What makes this situation particularly thorny is that energy forecasting equations are often used for policy analysis. Critics of a particular policy seem to be on stronger ground in attacking forecasts based on equations containing insignificant price terms—especially if the resultant analysis relies on price effects—than policy architects who claim that theory dictates that price terms be included. Thus while negative but statistically insignificant price effects might be in a long term study on theoretical grounds, public skepticism places short term policy studies based on statistically insignificant price effects in an unfavorable position.

A third constraint is that energy forecasts relate to macroeconomic variables. Since energy consumption is a derived demand, its level of usage is tied to personal income, industry production levels, and other variables, such as defense spending (for naptha-type jet fuel).

Finally, it is reasonable to impose a condition that short term models are not inconsistent with long term models. Naturally such models are not exactly the same; they differ in emphasis and focus. Weather has a significant short term impact but plays a small role in long term forecasts. However, annual long term models that do not account for annual weather effects in the estimation period will surely overemphasize price effects because the 1973–1975 period exhibited both higher annual prices and warmer annual weather. The forecasts still will be for "normal" weather, but the price coefficients will be affected. The equations presented here were compared to equations in FEA's Project Independence Blueprint, 1974. Essentially, the elasticities computed from the monthly model were the same as those in the annual model.

Data

There are three types of data: consumption data, price data, and macroeconomic activity data. All the consumption data are from the Bureau of Mines, *Mineral Industry Surveys*. All the price data are from the U.S. Department of Labor's Bureau of Labor Statistics Consumer Price Index (CPI) or Wholesale Price Index (WPI) series. Wholesale prices are used for middle distillate, residual, kerosene-based jet fuel, propane, and for all refined petroleum products (a proxy used whenever specific price data were not available). Retail prices for gasoline, weighted by regular and premium consumption including sales tax, are used. Personal income figures from the U.S. Department of Commerce's Bureau of Economic Analysis are used, and all industrial production indexes used are from Federal Reserve Board figures. Revenue passenger miles are from Civil Aeronautics Board *Air Carrier Traffic Statistics*. Figures for government purchases for national defense are from the Bureau of Economic Analysis series.

Methodology and Equations

Eight equations, (6.1) through (6.8), are used to produce the petroleum forecasts. All estimates have been made in logarithmic scale. Except for petrochemical feedstocks, all estimates are based on deseasonalized data.

We first estimated all prices in separate equations using a crude oil price as the identifying variable to reduce simultaneous bias. Since many equations are estimated over the years 1968 to 1974, we used dummy variables to capture the impact of supply restrictions during the embargo period. Lagged endogenous variables are included to make the model dynamic.

Deseasonalized data were used in the estimation process. An implicit assumption is that normal weather will occur during the forecast period. However, if abnormal weather should occur—or if the impact of abnormal weather is to be assessed before the fact—the following methodology is employed. Distillate, residual, and liquefied gases' seasonal factors obtained from the deseasonalization routine are regressed on heating degree day variables to determine elasticities for weather. The seasonal factors are then adjusted to simulate abnormal weather. The weather elasticities obtained from this process are: distillate heating degree day elasticity, 0.32; liquefied gases heating degree day elasticity, 0.23; and residual heating degree day elasticity, 0.18. This regression process assigns seasonal variation to nonweather (the intercept) and weather influences.

Because a lagged endogenous variable was included, price and economic activity elasticities over time can be generated. These are presented in Tables 6–1, 6–2, and 6–3. Finally, because lagged endogenous

Table 6–1
Petroleum Product Price Elasticities
(all price elasticities are negative values)

Product	Variable[a]	Equation	Impact	One Year	Two Years	Three Years	Long Run
Motor gasoline	P	(6.1)	0.186	0.304	0.378	0.425	0.505
Distillate	P	(6.2)	0.128	0.194	0.227	0.244	0.263
Residual	P	(6.3)	0.172	0.215	0.225	0.228	0.229
Kerosene-type jet fuel	P[b]	(6.4)	0.210	0.210	0.210	0.210	0.210
Liquefied gases	P	(6.7)	0.181	0.181	0.181	0.181	0.181
Other	P[c]	(6.8)	0.178	0.284	0.347	0.347	0.440
Weighted average for all products			0.132	0.188	0.218	0.240	0.264

[a]The motor gasoline elasticity, measured by retail average, was scaled down to produce its wholesale equivalent. P refers to the wholesale price of the petroleum product listed to its left. Except for residual, wholesale prices are deflated by the Wholesale Price Index (WPI). For residual, price is deflated by the price of fuels and related power in Eq. (6.3). (6.3).

[b]A lag structure associated with intertemporal changes in price elasticities was not chosen for kerosene-type fuel.

[c]To arrive at the elasticity for other petroleum products, the average wholesale refined product price was used.

Table 6-2
Dynamically Specified Economic Activity Elasticities

Product	Variable[a]	Equation	Impact	One Year	Two Years	Three Years	Long Run
Motor gasoline	Y	(6.1)	0.378	0.617	0.768	0.863	1.030
Distillate	M	(6.2)	0.831	1.257	1.475	1.587	1.705
Residual	E	(6.3)	1.395	1.742	1.828	1.850	1.857
Other	M	(6.8)	0.504	0.805	0.985	1.092	1.250

Table 6-3
Statically Specified Economic Activity Elasticities

Product	Variable	Equation	Impact
Kerosene-type jet fuel	T, R	(6.4)	0.781
Naphtha-type jet fuel	G	(6.5)	0.667
Petrochemical feedstocks	L	(6.6)	0.261
Liquefied gases	C	(6.7)	0.692

variables are used, Durbin-Watson statistics cannot be used to detect autocorrelation. Consequently, Cochrane-Orcutt transformations were made for all the equations, and a nonlinear least squares technique was then used to estimate the equations.

The equations for demand of motor gasoline (6.1), distillate fuel oil (6.2), residual fuel (6.3), kerosene-type jet fuel (6.4), naphtha-type jet fuel (6.5), liquefied gases (6.7), and other products (6.8) present deseasonalized estimates adjusted to reflect seasonal variations. The method used to obtain seasonal adjustments is borrowed from the Census Bureau's X-11 routine used in deseasonalizing data.[1] The estimation interval used in Eq. (6.1) is from March 1968 to December 1974.

$$DG_t = 0.727 - 0.186P_t + 0.378Y_t + 0.629DG_{t-1} \quad (6.1)$$
$$(3.2) \quad (-6.67) \quad (4.44) \quad (11.1)$$

$$-0.03A_t + 0.002S_t$$
$$(-3.7) \quad (0.98)$$

$$\bar{R}^2 = 0.94; \quad D.W. = 2.08; \quad S.E.E. = 0.022$$

where DG_t is the seasonally adjusted domestic demand for gasoline; P_t is the weighted retail price index of regular and premium gasoline (including sales tax) deflated by the CPI, estimated separately; Y_t is personal income deflated by the CPI; DG_{t-1} is demand lagged one year; A_t is a dummy variable that is one for the period November 1973 to April 1974, zero otherwise; and S_t is a dummy variable that equals DG_{t-1} for the period from November 1974 to April 1975, zero otherwise. In all equations

t-statistics are reported in parentheses below their coefficients. When actual data are regressed on predicted data for motor gasoline, the mean coefficient of determination is 0.95 and the standard error is 131M/BD.

When actual data are regressed on seasonal predictions for demand for distillate fuel oil, the mean coefficient of determination is 0.95 and the standard error is 180M/BD. The estimation interval used in predicting demand for distillate is from January 1967 to December 1974.

$$DD_t = 3.7 + 0.83M_t - 0.13P_t + 0.51DD_{t-1} \quad (6.2)$$
$$(5.3) \quad (5.96) \quad (-2.44) \quad (5.52)$$
$$+ 0.008S_t - 0.11A_t$$
$$(0.87) \quad (-2.9)$$
$$\bar{R}^2 = 0.73; \quad D.W. = 1.6; \quad S.E.E. = 0.065.$$

where DD_t is the seasonally adjusted demand for distillate fuel oil; M_t is the Federal Reserve Board index of manufacturing; P_t is the wholesale price index of middle distillate deflated by the WPI, estimated separately; DD_{t-1} is demand lagged for one year; S_t is a dummy variable that is equal to DD_{t-1} for the period December 1974 to March 1975, zero otherwise; and A_t is a dummy variable that is one for the period December 1973 to March 1974, zero otherwise.

When actual data for the demand for residual fuel are regressed on estimated demand, the mean coefficient of determination is 0.90 and the standard error is 133M/BD. The estimation interval used in Eq. (6.3) is from February 1970 to December 1974. The monthly demand for residual fuel is

$$DR_t = 4.57 - 0.17P_t + 1.19E_t + 0.25DR_{t-1} \quad (6.3)$$
$$(5.8) \quad (-3.73) \quad (6.68) \quad (2.07)$$
$$\bar{R}^2 = 0.73; \quad D.W. \ 2.22; \quad S.E.E. = 0.058$$

where DR_t is the seasonally adjusted monthly domestic demand for residual fuel; P_t is the wholesale price index of residual deflated by the wholesale price index of fuels and related power, estimated separately; E_t is the Federal Reserve Board production index of electricity, squared; and DR_{t-1} is demand lagged one year.

The equations used to estimate the monthly demand for kerosene-type jet fuel and naphtha-type jet fuel are presented below.

$$DK_t = 4.13 + 0.15T_t + 0.78R_t - 0.21P_t - 0.104A_t \quad (6.4)$$
$$(11.08) \quad (1.2) \quad (5.18) \quad (-3.99) \quad (-3.8)$$
$$\bar{R}^2 = 0.86; \quad D.W. = 2.13; \quad S.E.E. = 0.0596$$

where DK_t is the seasonally adjusted domestic demand for kerosene-type jet fuel; T_t is mail, express, the freight ton-miles in millions of ton-miles; R_t is revenue passenger-miles in billions of passenger-miles; P_t is the wholesale price index of light distillate fuel deflated by the WPI, estimated separately; and A_t is a dummy variable that is one for the period October 1973 to March 1974, zero otherwise. The estimation interval for Eq. (6.4) is from January 1967 to December 1974. When actual data for DK_t are regressed on DK_t, the $\bar{R}^2$ is 0.84 and the standard error is 43M/BD.

Equation (6.5) is estimated over the period from February 1968 to December 1974. The estimation of monthly domestic demand for naphtha-type jet fuel is the only equation that provides a better statistical fit when deseasonalized data are used. When (6.5) is converted to exponential form (from log form) and actual data are regressed on level predictions, the mean coefficient of determination is 0.9 and the standard error is 15M/BD.

$$DN_t = 12.44 + 0.67G_t - 1.7H_t \qquad (6.5)$$
$$(6.01) \quad (1.8) \quad (-8.7)$$

$$\bar{R}^2 = 0.71; \quad D.W. = 2.2; \quad S.E.E. = 0.096$$

where DN_t is the seasonally adjusted monthly demand for naphtha-type jet fuel; G_t is government military spending; and H_t is a monthly time variable.

The forecast for the monthly demand for petrochemical feedstocks is based on Eq. (6.6), the only one of eight where quantities were not seasonally adjusted. The full estimated equations, not reported here, included seasonal dummy variables for February, August, October, and December. For the equation reported here, quantities were estimated from January 1968 to December 1974.

$$DF_t = -4.5 + 0.261L_t + 1.65H_t \qquad (6.6)$$
$$(-0.27) \ (2.5) \quad (3.58)$$

$$\bar{R}^2 = 0.88; \quad D.W. = 1.86; \quad S.E.E. = 0.05$$

where DF_t is the domestic monthly demand for petrochemical feedstocks; L_t is the Federal Reserve Board index of plastics production; and H_t is a monthly time variable.

Equations (6.7) and (6.8) again provide deseasonalized estimates of demand for liquefied gases and other products, respectively. Demand for liquefied gases (DL_t) was estimated over the period from February 1970 to December 1974.

$$DL_t = \underset{(199.4)}{6.7} - \underset{(-2.87)}{0.18P_t} + \underset{(7.34)}{0.69C_t} - \underset{(-3.2)}{0.09A_t} \quad (6.7)$$

$$\bar{R}^2 = 0.47; \quad D.W. = 1.9; \quad S.E.E. = 0.06$$

where P_t is the wholesale price index of propane, deflated by the WPI, estimated separately; C_t is the Federal Reserve Board index of chemical production; and A_t is a dummy variable that takes on the value of one for the period from November 1973 to April 1974, zero otherwise. When DL_t was regressed on DL_t, the mean coefficient of determination was 0.93 and the standard error was 71M/BD.

The demand for other petroleum products (6.8) was estimated for February 1969 to December 1974. When actual data for demand were regressed on seasonal predictions, the $\bar{R}^2$ was 0.91 and the standard error was 62M/BD. Other petroleum products include items not estimated in Eqs. (6.1) through (6.7).

$$DO_t = \underset{(5.09)}{3.02} + \underset{(7.65)}{0.504M_t} - \underset{(-5.19)}{0.178P_t} + \underset{(7.59)}{0.596DO_{t-1}} \quad (6.8)$$

$$\bar{R}^2 = 0.76; \quad D.W. = 2.2; \quad S.E.E. = 0.03$$

where DO_t is the domestic monthly demand for other petroleum products; M_t is the Federal Reserve Board index of manufacturing; P_t is the wholesale price index of all petroleum products, deflated by the WPI, estimated separately; and DP_{t-1} is the demand for other products lagged one year.

Table 6–4 presents our estimates from the above eight equations for the last quarter of 1975 compared to reports made by the Bureau of Mines. Our forecasts were accurate. The only difficulty we encountered was predicting the split between distillate (6.2) and residual fuel oil (6.3).

Policy Implications and Conclusions

Equations (6.1) through (6.8) demonstrate that even in the near term, prices do matter. Consequently, policy alternatives that employ actions designed to change prices will change consumption levels. Moreover, these equations present one method of identifying reduced consumption resulting from warmer weather as well as from higher prices or from reduced economic activity. The years 1974 and 1975 not only exhibited higher energy prices but also had poor economic performances and mild weather. Future policy actions that view all the energy consumption

Table 6-4
Petroleum Product Detail Demand: Comparison of FEA Forecast with BOM Actual
(M/BD)

Product	January 1975	February 1975	March 1975	Average First Quarter	First-Quarter Percent Difference
Motor gasoline					
FEA forecast	5951	6021	6339	6106	−1.9
BOM actual	6238	6106	6327	6227	
Distillate					
FEA forecast	3932	3730	3162	3604	−2.0
BOM actual	3953	3805	3293	3680	
Residual					
FEA forecast	3324	3080	2888	3098	5.5
BOM actual	3257	2868	2678	2937	
Other					
FEA forecast	4808	4517	4311	4546	—
BOM actual	4763	4554	4231	4515	
Total					
FEA forecast	18075	17348	16700	17355	—
BOM actual	18211	17333	16529	17358	—

Note: The dashes indicate a difference of less than one percent.

reductions occurring in those years as the exclusive result of higher prices will be overestimating price effects. Similarly, conservation schemes that overlook price effects or abnormal weather overestimate the impact of voluntary actions.

Given demand estimates from the above-described econometric demand model, a linear programming supply model can be used to select a supply allocation that satisfies demand subject to constraints. For the eight products, five regions, and time periods a supply/demand balance is provided by the linear program. Subject to constraints enumerated below, an artificially constructed "cost" function was minimized. Costs are associated with (1) slack refining capacity, (2) product shortfalls in any region or time period, and (3) securing supplies from nonregional sources. A hierarchy of weights can be appropriately chosen to meet desired objectives.

Constraints relate to levels of stocks, refining capacity, interregional shipments, product yield patterns, blending ratios and transfers, import bounds, and disaggregation rules for product demand.

Given demand estimates, alternative scenarios can be examined to forecast shortfalls at current prices or products that might be expected to experience price increases. Supply disruptions or abnormal weather patterns can be examined also.

Note

1. Julius Shiskin, Allan H. Young, and John C. Musgrave, *The X–11 Variant of the Census Method II Seasonal Adjustment Program*, Bureau of the Census Technical Paper no. 15 (revised), (Washington, D.C.: U.S. Department of Commerce, 1967).

7

The Macroeconometric Implications of Alternative Energy Scenarios

A. Bradley Askin

Introduction

Effective energy policy cannot be established solely on the basis of energy sector analysis. Attention must also be given to the impacts energy has on other sectors of the economy. Such impacts require study for two separate reasons. One, the energy sector outcomes likely to be associated with particular energy policies can be accurately forecast only when the macroeconomic environments that both shape and are shaped by these outcomes are correctly forecast. Two, the macroeconomic environments implied by competing energy policies are important in their own right and merit consideration when one evaluates energy policy proposals.

Existing models deal inadequately with the linkages between the energy sector and other sectors of the economy. Macroeconometric models—even large scale models with substantial sectoral detail—presume the absence of supply side energy constraints owing to a demand side orientation.[a] Input–output models could handle such supply constraints to the extent that their interindustry production flows were sufficiently disaggregated, but invariably they include major energy producing industries within broader sectors owing to data limitations. In addition, input–output models do not realistically allow for input substitution possibilities that are particularly important in the long run. Finally, input–output models treat the determination of final demand superficially, sometimes ignoring it entirely. Most microeconomic models of the energy sector, or portions of it, employ exogenous macroeconomic variables, but none uses endogenous variables in a manner that permits analysis of the feedback effects the energy sector has on the economy.

Efforts to build sophisticated models that explicitly address the complex interactions between the energy sector and the rest of the economy have recently been initiated at the Federal Energy Administration (FEA) and elsewhere.[b] At FEA a project is in progress to incorporate new

---

[a]The Wharton model provides a partial exception to this statement, since it contains an imbedded input–output matrix. It does not qualify as a complete exception, however, because the interindustry transaction coefficients in the matrix do not distinguish between price and quantity effects. See [12] and [14].

[b]The Electric Power Research Institute has funded a project being conducted by Wharton Econometric Forecasting Associates, Inc. The most notable project completed to date is probably that funded by the Ford Foundation and others to develop the Hudson-Jorgenson model, which is described in [10].

energy sector data into an input-output matrix imbedded in a large scale, disaggregated macroeconometric model. Until such efforts prove successful, however, there is no alternative to exploring the economic impacts of proposed energy policies with ad hoc modifications of existing models and techniques. During the last two years FEA has employed several versions of such analysis to study the macroeconomic effects associated with various energy scenarios. This chapter describes the methodologies employed in these FEA analyses, points out their limitations, and presents forecasts of the economy in 1985 based on the analyses for a common set of energy scenarios.

Alternative Methodologies

General Framework

FEA has developed a set of models—known as the Project Independence Evaluation System (PIES)—that forecast future conditions in the energy sector at a given time under a variety of assumptions concerning energy and conservation policies, technology, and resource availability. PIES consists of an econometric demand model that explains quantity as a function of price and a fixed-point programming supply model with integrating framework that solves for equilibrium prices and quantities given demand elasticities derived from the demand model. Both the demand and supply models are regionally disaggregated and fuel specific; the supply model explicitly separates extraction, transportation, and processing costs. Among the main exogenous forces driving the demand model are several macroeconomic variables. The supply model integrating framework generates substantial information about energy prices, consumption, domestic production, and imports, along with limited information about cumulative capital needs.[c]

The integrating framework output produced by PIES for various energy scenarios provides a basis for examining the macroeconomic implications of those scenarios. Ideally, successive iterations of PIES and macroeconomic analyses should be employed to establish convergence or divergence between the macroeconomic forecasts used to drive PIES and implied by PIES, since these forecasts are likely to differ initially. To date, the same set of macroeconomic assumptions has been used to drive PIES for all FEA energy scenarios, and no iterations of PIES and macroeconomic analyses have been undertaken to test for convergence. Figure 7-1 is a flow chart depicting the use of PIES to analyze the macroeconomic implications of an energy scenario.

---

[c]PIES is described in [8, pp. A195–A282]. For critiques of PIES, see [9] and [11].

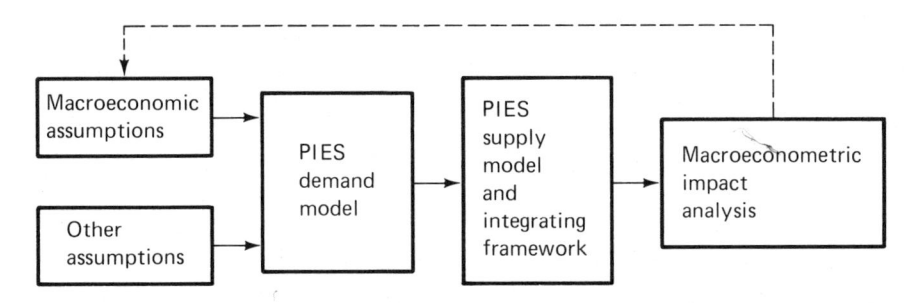

Figure 7-1. Flow Chart of PIES and Macroeconomic Analyses.

Three different, though similar, methodologies have been used to study the macroeconomic implications of alternative energy scenarios. All three approaches involve macroeconometric model simulations that treat prices as the major link between the energy sector and the economy in general. The methodologies differ in the way energy price changes are transmitted to other parts of the economy and in the way other information from PIES is handled. One method was developed in conjunction with Chase Econometric Associates, Inc., for implementation with the Chase macroeconomic model; the other two methods were developed in cooperation with Data Resources, Inc. (DRI), for implementation with the DRI macroeconometric model.[d]

Input–Output Pricing

The Chase methodology centers on a slightly modified version of the 185-sector Inforum input–output model, developed by Clopper Almon and others, that links PIES energy price information to prices in general in the Chase macroeconometric model.[e] First, PIES forecasts of eight energy prices in constant dollar terms for selected years are converted into current dollar terms on the basis of Chase's baseline forecast of the Consumer Price Index (CPI).[f] Second, current dollar forecasts are created for other years by interpolation. Third, the current dollar forecasts that result are compared with forecasts of the same energy prices prepared by

---

[d]The Chase macroeconometric model is described in [3]; the impact assessment methodology developed for implementation with the Chase macroeconometric model is described in [2]; the DRI macroeconometric model is described in [6]; and the impact assessment methodologies developed for implementation with the DRI macroeconometric model are described in [4] and [5].

[e]The version of Inforum developed by Clopper Almon and others is described in [1].

[f]The eight energy prices used are those of crude petroleum, gasoline, distillate oil, residual oil, other refined petroleum products, coal, natural gas, and electricity.

Chase in constructing its Inforum baseline solution. Fourth, the vector of percentage differences between these two sets of energy price forecasts for each year is multiplied by the inverse of the Inforum (I-A) matrix to compute price adjustment factors for all 185 sectors in Inforum. This last step yields adjustment factors for the eight energy prices different from the percentage differences originally found, so the computed adjustment factors for these eight energy prices are overridden with the original deviations.[g]

The price adjustment factors corresponding to the 185 sectors in Inforum provide a means to adjust prices in the Chase macroeconometric model. An adjustment factor for each price variable appearing in the macroeconometric model is calculated as a weighted average of the appropriate Inforum price adjustment factors with a bridge equation. Then these macroeconomic adjustment factors are multiplied by the values assigned to the price variables in the macroeconometric model baseline solution to compute absolute price changes. Finally, the absolute price changes are employed as add factors in the macroeconometric model.

Although prices act as the main force in Chase macroeconometric model simulations, they are not the only force. Imports and investment in both plant and equipment are also adjusted on the basis of PIES integrating framework output. Petroleum imports—a separate category of final demand in the Chase macroeconometric model—are treated as an exogenous variable and adjusted to coincide with the sum of various types of petroleum imports reported by PIES. Investment expenditures for plant and equipment are modified with a complicated process similar to the one just described for prices. The process produces add factors intended to reconcile Inforum baseline investment forecasts with PIES cumulative capital requirement forecasts.

Stage of Process Pricing

The first DRI methodology was designed for the 1974 DRI macroeconometric model, but it can be used with other versions of the model with some modifications. It employs a stage of process price model developed by DRI to link PIES energy price information to prices in general as modeled in the 1974 DRI macroeconometric model.[h] First, the same PIES forecasts of eight energy prices in constant dollar terms for selected years utilized by the input-output pricing methodology are con-

---

[g]The adjustment factors for the eight energy prices are reset at their original values on the assumption that PIES correctly forecasts changes in these prices. Under such an assumption, not to reset these adjustment factors would be to double count energy price changes.

[h]The stage of process price model developed by DRI is described in [7].

verted into price index form with 1967 the base year, that is, 1967 = 1.0. This is done on the basis of historical energy price data and DRI's baseline forecast of the CPI. Second, price index forecasts are created for other years by interpolation. Third, appropriate weighted averages of the price index forecasts that result are employed to construct forecasts of four energy price indexes appearing in the stage of process price model developed by DRI. Fourth, the stage of process price model is simulated using these four energy price index forecasts as exogenous variables. Fifth, adjustment factors are found for all price indexes in the stage of process price model by comparing their values in the stage of process price model simulation just described with their values in DRI's baseline solution of the stage of process price model.

The price index adjustment factors from the stage of process price model provide a means to adjust prices in the 1974 DRI macroeconometric model. An adjustment factor for each price variable appearing in the 1974 DRI macroeconometric model is computed as a weighted average of the appropriate stage of process price model adjustment factors with a bridge equation. Next, these adjustment factors are multiplied by the values assigned to the price variables in a standard 1974 DRI macroeconometric model solution to compute absolute price changes. Finally, a new simulation of the macroeconometric model is run. This simulation can be run with prices either exogenous or adjusted by add factors, whereas only the latter option is feasible with the Chase methodology.

By itself, the stage of process price model provides no basis for addressing nonprice energy impacts on the economy. Imports are adjusted in all DRI macroeconometric model simulations with an algorithm discussed in the next subsection on the second DRI methodology. Investment is not adjusted for the reasons given in the next subsection.

Direct Adjustment Pricing

The 1975 DRI macroeconometric model differs significantly from the Chase macroeconometric model and earlier versions of the DRI macroeconometric model in that it contains an explicit energy price variable—the Wholesale Price Index (WPI) for fuel and related products and for power—which affects other prices and the general price level.[i] The second DRI methodology was designed to exploit this new loop within the DRI macroeconometric model by directly linking PIES energy price information to the WPI for fuel and related products and for power

---

[i]The relationship that the WPI for fuel and related products and for power bears to other price variables in the DRI macroeconometric model is described in [6, pp. 59–68].

in the 1975 DRI macroeconometric model and letting the macroeconometric model determine how other prices react.

The first two steps in the linking procedure are identical to those of the stage of process pricing methodology. Next, a weighted average of the energy price index forecasts so formed is computed as a proxy for the WPI for fuels and related products and for power. This proxy is a good one, because the WPI for fuel and related products and for power is a Bureau of Labor Statistics series, constructed from individual price indexes, that covers energy categories roughly the same as the eight PIES prices.[j] Finally, the proxy forecast of the WPI for fuel and related products and for power is used to generate a new simulation for the 1975 DRI macroeconometric model.

Like the stage of process pricing methodology, the direct adjustment pricing methodology ignores nonprice energy effects on the economy. Separate algorithms are needed to take these impacts into account. Crude petroleum imports and refined petroleum product imports appear as exogenous variables in the DRI macroeconometric model and are simply assigned new values based on the sums of various categories of petroleum imports reported by PIES. The procedure is consistent with that used in the input–output pricing methodology. No attempt is made to adjust investment for two reasons. First, the input–output pricing methodology investment adjustments suffer from serious problems, which are discussed in the next section. Second, much less information on which to base such adjustments is available with the DRI methodologies than with the input–output methodology, where the Inforum model provides considerable sectoral detail concerning investment.

Limitations

Common Problems

The three methodologies just described share several significant shortcomings. Perhaps the most serious involves the heavy reliance placed on prices while production levels are ignored in linking the energy sector to the rest of the economy. As Figure 7–2 shows, a price change stemming from a demand shift moves output in the opposite direction than does the same price change stemming from a supply shift. Looking exclusively at prices misses this distinction and results in an analysis based on incomplete information.

Unfortunately, little can be done to overcome this problem. The

---

[j]The weighted average of the eight energy price indexes is computed with Bureau of Labor Statistics weights found in [13, pp. 27–28].

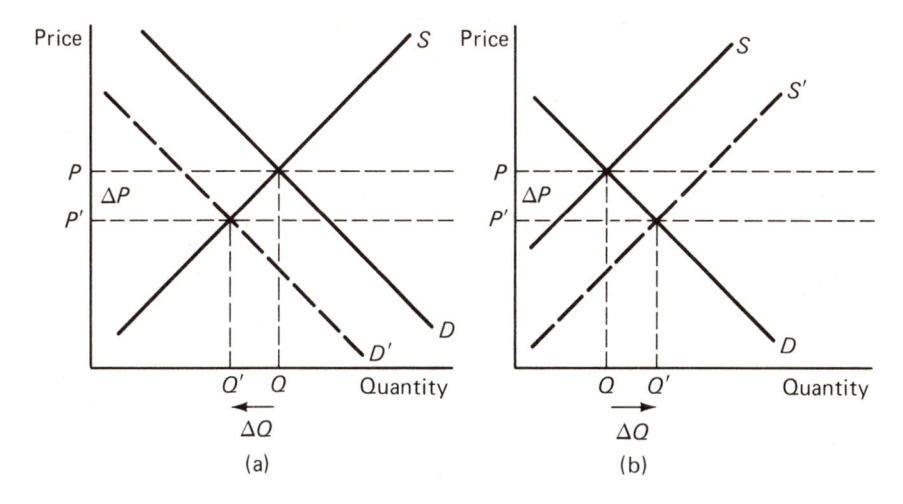

Figure 7-2. Quantity Impacts Associated with the Same Price Changes Induced by Demand versus Supply Shifts. (a) Demand Shift; (b) Supply Shift.

Chase and DRI macroeconometric models have typically Keynesian final demand orientations incapable of distinguishing between energy sector price changes induced by demand versus supply shifts. For the most part, these models treat price changes as movements along demand curves and ignore supply constraints. Moreover, they employ final demand categories that bear little or no direct relation to energy—with the exception of personal consumption expenditures for gasoline and oil—so that exogenous adjustments and constraints cannot be employed to represent energy sector production level changes. This makes it virtually impossible to take into account nonprice supply constraints, output changes associated with price changes, or market structure and regulation changes when constructing linkages from the energy sector to the rest of the economy.

As noted earlier, successive iterations of PIES and macroeconomic analyses are desirable to establish convergence or divergence of the macroeconomic forecasts used to drive PIES and implied by PIES. The failure to undertake more than one iteration not only leaves the convergence or divergence issue unsettled, but also yields erroneous macroeconomic impact estimates. In the case of convergence, the failure to iterate probably overstates the differences among alternative energy scenarios. Consider two PIES scenarios, one with high energy prices and another with low energy prices. The former scenario will produce a higher general price level and more rapid inflation, which in turn will reduce real GNP and retard economic growth with both the Chase and DRI macroeconometric models. If second round PIES simulations based on such first round macroeconomic impacts were run, the lower real GNP associated with the high energy price scenario would normally depress the demand for energy in the high energy price scenario relative to the low energy price scenario and yield energy price differences between the revised PIES scenarios that were smaller than the energy price differences between the original PIES scenarios. A second round macroeconometric comparison of the new PIES scenarios would then reveal smaller impact differences than the first round comparison. By similar reasoning, subsequent iterations of PIES and macroeconomic analyses could be expected to yield still different impact estimates that narrowed the gap between the two scenarios even further.[k]

To link the energy sector to the rest of the economy properly, variables must be defined and measured in consistent fashion at all stages of the linking procedure. Yet a paucity of good energy data and the adoption of unusual conventions in PIES that cannot be carried over into the Chase and DRI macroeconometric models seriously limit the extent to which many energy variables can be handled consistently. The treatment of natural gas in the direct adjustment pricing methodology provides an excellent illustration of the problems encountered.

PIES provides information on the city gate price of natural gas sold in the interstate market, whereas the WPI for fuel and related products and for power used in the 1975 DRI macroeconometric model is based on the wellhead price of natural gas sold in the intrastate market. Reconciling these two different prices of natural gas is not feasible. First, good data on the price of natural gas sold in the intrastate market are not available on a national average basis. Second, data on the processing and transmission costs incurred between wellhead and city gate are not available in reliable form on a national average basis. Similar inconsistencies are the rule, not the exception, for the majority of variables regardless of which methodology is considered.

Different levels of government expenditures and investment should be assigned to different energy scenarios. Government expenditures will be influenced by changes in energy policies that involve subsidies, direct intervention, or taxes, and by changes in energy prices that affect the cost of energy.[l] Investment must vary among scenarios to produce the differ-

---

[k]Two points must be emphasized. First, convergence occurs within individual scenarios and does not imply elimination of all differences among the macroeconomic impact forecasts for alternative scenarios. Second, changes in other variables between iterations could have destabilizing effects that more than offset the effects changes in the real GNP have. This would lead to divergence instead of convergence. In this case the failure to iterate would understate the differences among alternative scenarios.

[l]A broad definition of government expenditures, in terms of the impact that the government surplus or deficit has on the economy, is implied here rather than the narrower definition normally used.

ent energy sector production capacities they imply, unless there is a dollar-for-dollar offsetting variation in nonenergy investment. Not making adjustments to government expenditures can be at least partially excused by the secondary importance such adjustments are likely to have, particularly since PIES provides no information about government expenditures. The treatment of investment is more important, however, and cannot be dismissed so lightly.

Once it has generated integrating framework estimates of future energy production, PIES multiplies these estimates by fixed capital-output coefficients selected on the basis of historical experience to forecast cumulative capital needs in individual energy industries. Energy sector investment forecasts are then derived from these cumulative capital needs with other FEA models after making appropriate assumptions about current capital stocks, depreciation rates, construction lead times, and the like. At one extreme, the input–output pricing methodology treats the resulting energy sector investment forecasts as a net increase in total investment. This approach assumes that crowding out occurs only to the extent that general economic conditions affect total investment in Chase macroeconometric model simulations. Several modifications of the FEA energy sector investment forecasts were required before Chase macroeconometric model simulations that made economic sense could be generated.[m] At the other extreme, the other two methodologies ignore the energy sector investment forecasts implied by PIES. This approach assumes complete crowding out except for the effects that general economic conditions have on investment in DRI macroeconometric model simulations. The truth undoubtedly lies somewhere between these two polar cases, but the lack of sectoral detail on investment in the Chase and DRI macroeconometric models precludes empirical analysis via explicit adjustments to energy sector investment to settle the issue.

Specific Problems

In addition to their common shortcomings, the three methodologies suffer unique deficiencies with respect to the price linkages from the energy sector to the rest of the economy. For example, the input–output pricing methodology assumes fixed factor proportions. This assumption ignores input substitution possibilities and results in overstating the impacts that increased energy costs have on other prices.

The stage of process pricing methodology suffers from two flaws.

---

[m] The FEA models used to generate the energy sector investment forecasts are based on logistic curves. Given the limited number of years for which PIES forecasts are available, a large number of such curves could be found to allocate the flow of investment over time. Problems arose in selecting a particular curve that led to reasonable macroeconometric results.

First, the stage of process price model developed by DRI is based on reduced form equations that have less explanatory power than is desirable for long run forecasting. Consequently, long run impact estimates based on the model cannot be considered reliable. Second, the model contains a number of lags that cause it to underpredict price changes when linked to the DRI macroeconometric model. Preliminary tests of the stage of process model used by itself yielded approximately the same CPI and WPI forecasts as the direct adjustment pricing methodology. When linked to the 1974 DRI macroeconometric model in tests, however, the lags in the stage of process price model interacted with the lags in the macroeconometric model to yield CPI and WPI forecasts that did not reflect even the direct effects of energy price variations on those two price indexes.

The direct adjustment pricing methodology treats changes in all energy prices as mere scalars of one another by using a simple weighted average of individual energy prices to alter the WPI for fuel and related products and for power in the 1975 DRI macroeconometric model. Consequently, this methodology cannot distinguish among the impacts that changes in different energy prices would have on relative prices or on the structure, and thus performance, of the economy.

Forecasts of the Economy in 1985

Scenarios

FEA examined the long run implications of four major energy strategies with PIES in *Project Independence Report* [8]. Separate PIES simulations covering the individual years 1977, 1980, and 1985 were run for each strategy, with a world crude petroleum price fixed first at $7 and then $11 per barrel in constant 1973 dollars. The four strategies considered were: (1) business as usual (BAU), with no major policy initiatives; (2) conservation (Con.), based on mandatory nonprice demand reduction programs; (3) accelerated development (Acc. Dev.), relying on federal subsidies and relaxation of environmental controls to encourage the development of new energy supplies; and (4) conservation and accelerated development (Con./Acc. Dev.), involving both demand and supply actions.

Three sets of macroeconometric simulations covering the years 1975 through 1985 have been run for the eight scenarios formed by the four strategies and the two world crude petroleum prices. One set employs the input–output pricing methodology with the Chase macroeconometric model. Another set utilizes the direct adjustment pricing methodology with the 1975 DRI macroeconometric model. The third set uses a modified version of the direct adjustment pricing methodology in which personal consumption expenditures for gasoline and oil are treated as exogenous variables in the 1975 DRI macroeconometric model on the basis of information generated by PIES.[n] No simulations are presented for the stage of process pricing model owing to the obsolescence of the 1974 DRI macroeconometric model and the price impact underestimation problem discussed in the previous section.

The forecasts generated with the three sets of macroeconometric simulations must be analyzed with care, because they reflect both differences among methodologies and differences between the Chase and DRI baseline forecasts. In the tables that follow, all forecasts are stated in terms of departures from the $11 BAU scenario forecast generated with the methodology in question to minimize the influence of baseline forecast differences and focus on the differences among methodologies.

Results

Tables 7–1 through 7–5 compare the 1985 forecasts of selected variables generated by the three sets of macroeconometric simulations in the eight alternative scenarios described above. Several points can be made on the basis of these tables. Undertaking a more elaborate analysis based on information for additional years and variables is deferred to another study that goes beyond the scope of this one.

Table 7–1 shows that going from any $11 scenario to the comparable $7 scenario has a bigger price level impact than going from one $11 or $7 scenario to another $11 or $7 scenario, respectively, regardless of which methodology or price index is considered. This suggests that changes in the world price of crude petroleum have a potentially larger impact on price levels than does the choice among domestic energy strategies. Table 7–1 also reveals that energy price changes—measured by the WPI for fuel and related products and for power—uniformly lead to larger changes in the WPI than in either the implicit GNP deflator or the CPI, with no consistent pattern of changes emerging between the latter two indexes. This implies that energy price changes may have smaller long run impacts on price levels at successive stages of production as they work their way through the economy to final demand goods and services. Prices in general respond more to energy prices with the two direct adjustment

---

[n]PIES information on gasoline and oil prices and production are used to generate gasoline and oil sales forecasts. These sales forecasts are then converted into forecasts of personal consumption expenditures for gasoline and oil on the assumption that consumers will continue to purchase the same proportion of total gasoline and oil sold as they have on average in the recent past.

Table 7-1
Percent Differences in 1985 Price Levels between Other Scenarios and the $11 BAU Scenario

Scenario	Input-Output Pricing Methodology			Direct Adjustment Pricing Methodology			Modified Direct Adjustment Pricing Methodology			WPI for Fuel and Related Products and for Power
	Implicit GNP Deflator	CPI	WPI	Implicit GNP Deflator	CPI	WPI	Implicit GNP Deflator	CPI	WPI	
$11 BAU	NA	NA	NA	NA	NA	NA	NA	NA	NA	NA
$11 Con.	−1.24	−1.00	−1.19	0.53	0.48	−0.61	0.10	−0.22	−0.65	−1.85
$11 Acc. Dev.	−0.57	−0.20	−1.67	−0.20	−0.22	−2.26	0.30	0.30	−2.27	−6.75
$11 Con./Acc. Dev.	−2.08	−1.84	−2.83	−0.03	0.15	−3.52	−0.30	−0.41	−3.53	−9.84
$7 BAU	−4.46	−3.08	−6.00	−8.14	−7.30	−10.85	−7.87	−6.96	−10.79	−22.15
$7 Con.	−5.00	−3.41	−6.33	−7.91	−7.12	−11.71	−8.23	−7.62	−11.73	−24.34
$7 Acc. Dev.	−3.50	−2.61	−5.80	−7.75	−7.05	−10.89	−7.51	−6.77	−10.79	−22.46
$7 Con./Acc. Dev.	−5.06	−3.81	−7.79	−7.49	−6.82	−12.40	−7.87	−7.40	−12.41	−26.28

Source: Author's estimates.

Note: NA = not applicable. The WPI for fuels and related products and for power is used as one variable driving the DRI macroeconometric model and takes on the same values in both the direct adjustment pricing methodology and the modified direct adjustment pricing methodology; it does not appear in the Chase macroeconometric model and is not used in the input-output pricing methodology.

pricing methodologies than with the input–output pricing methodology. Experience gained in running a variety of macroeconometric simulations based on identical, non-PIES energy inputs indicates that this reflects greater price responsiveness in the DRI macroeconometric model than in the Chase macroeconometric model, not differences in the linkage methodologies.

The real GNP impacts reported in Table 7–2 for the two direct adjustment pricing methodologies are highly correlated with the price level impacts reported in Table 7–1. Once again, going from any $11 scenario to the comparable $7 scenario always has a larger impact on real GNP than going from one $11 or $7 scenario to another $11 or $7 scenario, respectively. The real GNP impacts for some scenarios are quite sizable in absolute terms, exceeding $50 billion in 1958 dollars, but in percent terms they are usually smaller than the price level effects with which they are associated.

The real GNP impacts reported in Table 7–2 for the input–output pricing methodology do not always follow the same pattern as the price level impacts reported in Table 7–1. Whereas the two direct adjustment pricing methodologies assume that investment responds only to economic

Table 7–2
Differences in 1985 Real GNP Levels Measured in Billions of 1958 Dollars between Other Scenarios and the $11 BAU Scenario

Scenario	Input-Output Pricing Methodology	Direct Adjustment Pricing Methodology	Modified Direct Adjustment Pricing Methodology
$11 BAU	NA	NA	NA
$11 Con.	8.8 (0.75)	6.4 (0.52)	0.1 (0.01)
$11 Acc. Dev.	17.0 (1.45)	14.5 (1.19)	14.1 (1.16)
$11 Con./Acc. Dev.	22.9 (1.96)	20.4 (1.67)	17.7 (1.45)
$7 BAU	19.6 (1.67)	36.9 (3.02)	41.3 (3.39)
$7 Con.	25.5 (2.18)	44.5 (3.64)	36.9 (3.03)
$7 Acc. Dev.	32.6 (2.78)	45.1 (3.69)	49.5 (4.06)
$7 Con./Acc. Dev.	44.7 (3.82)	56.6 (4.63)	50.8 (4.17)

Source: Author's estimates.
Note: NA = not applicable; percent differences in parentheses.

conditions in general, the input–output pricing methodology employs add factor adjustments to reflect the important role played by energy sector investment incentives. Lowering the world price of crude petroleum from $11 per barrel to $7 per barrel now encourages petroleum imports at the expense of domestic production and investment. Similarly, adopting a conservation strategy decreases the demand for energy as shown in part (a) of Figure 7–2 and discourages investment, while adopting an accelerated development strategy increases the supply of energy as shown in part (b) of Figure 7–2 and encourages investment.

Table 7–3 on real investment shows clearly that energy sector investment incentives affect fixed private nonresidential investment sufficiently with the input–output pricing methodology to significantly alter the pattern of total investment impacts from that reported for the two direct adjustment pricing methodologies. As can be seen, in fact, the total investment impacts are affected enough with the input–output pricing methodology to yield a pattern of real GNP impacts that violates the pattern of price level impacts for the $11 versus $7 scenarios.

High real GNP levels are normally associated with low unemployment rates and high capacity utilization rates, yet this is frequently not the case with the real GNP impacts reported in Table 7–2 and the unemployment rate and capacity utilization rate impacts reported in Table 7–4. The capacity utilization rate impacts for the input–output pricing methodology are perverse in five scenarios, while both the unemployment rate and the capacity utilization rate impacts for the two direct adjustment pricing methodologies are perverse in all four $7 scenarios. No explanation for the anomalies can be offered, but they highlight the need for caution when interpreting the impact estimates shown in the tables.

The effects of treating personal consumption expenditures for gasoline and oil as exogenous on the basis of information from PIES can be seen by comparing the real personal consumption impacts reported for the two direct adjusting pricing methodologies in Table 7–5. The exogenous personal consumption expenditures for gasoline and oil imposed with the modified direct adjustment pricing methodology have more intuitive appeal in terms of what would be expected for the various scenarios than do the endogenous ones determined by the 1975 DRI macroeconometric model with the original direct adjustment pricing methodology. The choice between the two approaches makes little difference with respect to the other impacts reported in Tables 7–1 through 7–4, although it does with respect to the total personal consumption expenditures reported in Table 7–5. This suggests that imposing exogenous quantity impacts will not significantly improve overall impact estimates when relatively unimportant final demand components are involved.

Table 7-3
Differences in 1985 Real Investment Levels Measured in Billions of 1958 Dollars between Other Scenarios and the $11 BAU Scenario

Scenarios	Input–Output Pricing Methodology — Fixed Private Nonresidential Investment	Input–Output Pricing Methodology — Gross Private Domestic Investment	Direct Adjustment Pricing Methodology — Fixed Private Nonresidential Investment	Direct Adjustment Pricing Methodology — Gross Private Domestic Investment	Modified Direct Adjustment Pricing Methodology — Fixed Private Nonresidential Investment	Modified Direct Adjustment Pricing Methodology — Gross Private Domestic Investment
$11 BAU	NA	NA	NA	NA	NA	NA
$11 Con.	−2.7 (−1.84)	2.1 (1.13)	0.1 (0.07)	0.1 (0.06)	−0.3 (0.22)	−0.2 (−0.11)
$11 Acc. Dev.	5.4 (3.69)	6.1 (3.28)	1.9 (1.40)	2.5 (1.42)	1.8 (1.33)	2.4 (1.36)
$11 Con./Acc. Dev.	1.2 (0.82)	6.2 (3.34)	2.4 (1.77)	3.7 (2.10)	2.4 (1.77)	4.1 (2.33)
$7 BAU	−5.1 (−3.48)	1.8 (0.97)	12.8 (9.42)	20.5 (11.62)	12.9 (9.50)	20.7 (11.74)
$7 Con.	−6.1 (−4.17)	4.3 (2.32)	13.0 (9.57)	20.2 (11.45)	13.0 (9.57)	20.0 (11.34)
$7 Acc. Dev.	6.0 (4.10)	10.0 (5.39)	12.4 (9.12)	19.4 (11.00)	12.7 (9.35)	19.8 (11.23)
$7 Con./Acc. Dev.	2.9 (1.98)	10.3 (5.55)	13.7 (10.08)	20.3 (11.51)	13.8 (10.16)	21.5 (12.20)

Source: Author's estimates.
Note: NA = not applicable; percent differences in parentheses.

Table 7-4
Percentage Point Differences in 1985 Unemployment Rates and Capacity Utilization Rates for Manufacturing between Other Scenarios and the $11 BAU Scenarios

Scenario	Input–Output Pricing Methodology Unemployment Rates	Input–Output Pricing Methodology Capacity Utilization Rates	Direct Adjustment Pricing Methodology Unemployment Rates	Direct Adjustment Pricing Methodology Capacity Utilization Rates	Modified Direct Adjustment Pricing Methodology Unemployment Rates	Modified Direct Adjustment Pricing Methodology Capacity Utilization Rates
$11 BAU	NA	NA	NA	NA	NA	NA
$11 Con.	−0.1	0.31	−0.1	0.5	0.1	0.6
$11 Acc. Dev.	−0.3	0.07	−0.2	0.9	−0.3	0.8
$11 Con./Acc. Dev.	−0.3	−0.50	−0.4	1.4	−0.3	1.8
$7 BAU	−0.3	−0.48	0.4	−1.0	0.3	−1.2
$7 Con.	−0.3	−0.46	0.3	−0.8	0.4	−0.6
$7 Acc. Dev.	−0.5	−0.79	0.3	−0.6	0.2	−0.6
$7 Con./Acc. Dev.	−0.6	−0.38	0.1	−0.4	0.2	0.0

Source: Author's estimates.

Note: NA = not applicable. Each tenth of a percentage point change in the 1985 unemployment rate is equivalent to between 107,000 and 110,000 jobs in all the macroeconometric simulations underlying this table.

Table 7-5
Differences in 1985 Real Personal Consumption Expenditure Levels Measured in Billions of 1958 Dollars between Other Scenarios and the $11 BAU Scenario

Scenarios	Input–Output Pricing Methodology — Personal Consumption Expenditures for Gasoline and Oil	Input–Output Pricing Methodology — Total Personal Consumption Expenditures	Direct Adjustment Pricing Methodology — Personal Consumption Expenditures for Gasoline and Oil	Direct Adjustment Pricing Methodology — Total Personal Consumption Expenditures	Modified Direct Adjustment Pricing Methodology — Personal Consumption Expenditures for Gasoline and Oil	Modified Direct Adjustment Pricing Methodology — Total Personal Consumption Expenditures
$11 BAU	NA	NA	NA	NA	NA	NA
$11 Con.	−0.8 (−2.43)	0.4 (0.18)	0.2 (0.70)	4.3 (0.53)	−4.8 (−18.75)	−2.8 (−0.35)
$11 Acc. Dev.	−1.0 (−3.04)	4.2 (0.54)	0.5 (1.72)	9.0 (1.11)	0.6 (2.34)	8.7 (1.08)
$11 Con./Acc. Dev.	−1.0 (−3.04)	8.3 (1.07)	0.7 (2.46)	12.6 (1.55)	−3.6 (−14.06)	7.0 (0.87)
$7 BAU	4.4 (13.37)	23.5 (3.04)	1.0 (3.51)	13.4 (1.65)	3.9 (15.23)	17.9 (2.21)
$7 Con.	3.4 (10.33)	22.8 (2.95)	1.2 (4.21)	17.4 (2.14)	−3.4 (−13.28)	11.1 (1.37)
$7 Acc. Dev.	3.2 (9.73)	24.6 (3.18)	1.2 (4.21)	17.5 (2.15)	3.9 (15.23)	21.8 (2.70)
$7 Con./Acc. Dev.	3.5 (10.64)	32.0 (4.13)	1.6 (5.61)	23.5 (2.89)	−3.3 (−12.89)	17.2 (2.13)

Source: Author's estimates.

Note: NA = not applicable; percentage differences in parentheses. Personal consumption expenditures for gasoline and oil are deflated by the CPI for gasoline and oil, not by the implicit GNP deflator for gasoline and oil, in the input–output pricing methodology.

Concluding Remarks

FEA designed the eight scenarios considered in the previous section to represent a reasonable set of possible energy futures. The macroeconometric forecasts presented for those futures demonstrate a genuine need to consider economic impacts on the rest of the economy when choosing which future to seek. The general price levels forecasted for 1985 differ among some of the scenarios by as much as 10 percent. The real GNP levels forecasted for 1985 differ among selected scenarios by as much as $50 billion in 1958 dollars. Such price level and real GNP level differences are equivalent to annual rates of inflation and economic growth that differ throughout the 1975 to 1985 period by 1 percent and 0.5 percent, respectively.

For the most part, the different methodologies used in this chapter produce broadly consistent impact estimates in Tables 7-1 through 7-5. Nevertheless, these methodologies must be rated less than satisfactory. First, they suffer from serious limitations as discussed earlier. Second, they lead to point estimates of the impacts expected, for which no reliability or bias measures can be constructed except on an ex post basis. Third, they do not give much insight into what goes on in individual sectors of the economy or of structural changes in the economy. The investment of more time, effort, and money is needed to develop improved methodologies and models if the long run impacts that energy has on the economy are to be understood fully.

References

[1] Almon, Clopper Jr., Margaret B. Buckler, Lawrence M. Hurwitz, and Thomas C. Reimbold. *1985: Interindustry Forecasts of the American Economy.* Lexington, Mass.: Lexington Books, D.C. Heath and Company, 1974.

[2] Chase Econometric Associates, Inc. "Evaluating the Economic Impact of Alternative Energy Scenarios: Methodology Report." Mimeographed. Bala Cynwyd, Pa. October 1975.

[3] ———. "The Chase Econometrics Macro Model." Mimeographed. Bala Cynwyd, Pa. 1975.

[4] Data Resources, Inc. "An Energy Price Impact Model." Mimeographed. Lexington, Mass. October, 1974.

[5] ———. "Measuring the Impacts of Energy Prices on Other Prices: Methodology Employed in the Stages of Processing Model." Mimeographed. Lexington, Mass. 1975.

[6] ———. "The Data Resources Quarterly Model: Operations Overview." Mimeographed. Lexington, Mass. May 1975.

[7] Earl, Paul H., and Nancy E. Kennedy. "A Disaggregated Approach to Forecasting Prices." In Paul H. Earl, ed., *Analysis of Inflation*. Lexington, Mass.: Lexington Books, D.C. Heath and Company, 1975. Pp. 129–169.

[8] Federal Energy Administration. *Project Independence Report*. Washington, D.C.: U.S. Government Printing Office, 1974.

[9] Hausman, Jerry A. "Project Independence Report: An Appraisal of U.S. Energy Needs Up to 1985." *Bell Journal of Economics and Management Science* 6, no. 2 (Autumn 1975): 517–551.

[10] Hudson, Edward A., and Dale W. Jorgenson. "U.S. Energy Policy and Economic Growth, 1975–2000." *Bell Journal of Economics and Management Science* 5, no. 2 (Autumn 1974): 461–514.

[11] M.I.T. Energy Laboratory Policy Study Group. "The FEA Project Independence Report: An Analytical Assessment and Evaluation." Mimeographed. Cambridge, Mass. May 1975.

[12] Preston, R.S. "The Wharton Long Term Model: Input–Output within the Context of a Macro Forecasting Model." *International Economic Review* 16, no. 1 (February 1975): 3–19.

[13] U.S. Department of Labor, Bureau of Labor Statistics. *Wholesale Prices and Price Indexes Supplement*. Washington, D.C.: U.S. Government Printing Office, 1974.

[14] Wharton Econometric Forecasting Associates, Inc. "Annual and Industrial Model Equations." Mimeographed. Philadelphia, Pa. June 1975.

8

Alternative Energy Policies' Impact on Industry Price Behavior

*Paul H. Earl and
Steven G. Phillips*

In the past several years, energy availability and inflation have joined unemployment as major concerns of decision-makers in the United States. Of the several important tradeoffs within and among these areas, energy availability versus inflation has been of particular concern. Increasing energy supply and/or decreasing energy demand can be expected to have a significant impact on inflation. The direction and magnitude of the impact depends on the policy choices made and the prices considered. This chapter provides some insight into the different impacts on inflation of several energy policy alternatives (scenarios) at a relatively low level of aggregation of the U.S. economy.

This chapter examines four policy alternatives: (1) conservation—reducing the quantity of energy demanded; (2) accelerated development—increasing the quantity of energy supplied; (3) combined conservation and accelerated development—reducing energy demanded and increasing energy supplied; and (4) business as usual—maintaining status quo. Each policy choice is evaluated under the alternative assumptions that crude oil currently costs either $7 or $11 per barrel. The first three policy choices are compared to the fourth, business as usual, which is treated as a base case. These alternatives are examined through 1985 with the Data Resources Inflation Monitoring Service (DRIMS) Model, which depends on the Data Resources Macro Model to provide exogenous variables.

The Model

The model employed is of the stages of processing type and concentrates on the intermediate stages with particular emphasis on durable materials, components, and construction materials. Several crude material prices (e.g., coal, iron, ore, scrap, sand and gravel, petroleum) affect various intermediate material prices (e.g., iron and steel, aluminum, hardware, insulation material), which in turn affect final product prices (e.g., machinery and equipment categories, tires, trucks, electronic instruments).

The two preparatory steps in simulating with this model are (1) adapting the model to the particular simulation and (2) obtaining a fully consistent set of exogenous variables for the simulation. Written into the model are ways to get results of the effect of lower stages of processing prices on higher ones (including indirect effects of energy price changes). The method must be altered to account for the direct effect of energy price changes on each price since energy is used in production of all commodities in the model. This direct effect is entered into the model through an adjustment factor:

$$AF = \alpha * CRUDE + \beta * COAL + \lambda * NATLGAS + \delta * ELECTRICITY + \epsilon * OTHER$$

where *CRUDE, COAL*, etc., are percent changes in the price indexes of the named energy sources, and *OTHER* is the percent change in the price index of refined petroleum products (gasoline, distillates, residual fuel, lubricants, and petroleum wax [WPI057]). The percent change form is used because the price forecasting equations in the model are specified in this form. The coefficients α through ϵ are different for each price since the different energy sources vary in importance across products. For example, electricity has a weight of 0.013 in WPI1013 (steel mill products) and a weight of only 0.004 in WPI1130 (metal-working machinery and equipment) due to greater use of electricity in steel-making than in producing metal-working machines. These coefficients are simply the input–output coefficients for the appropriate industry column and energy source row of the *Input–Output Structure of the United States: 1967*. Only coefficients greater than or equal to 0.001 are entered; elsewhere coefficients are zero. We also depend on the price model to construct energy price equations for intermediate and final fuels. These equations feed into the model through their effect at the cruder processing stages (see the appendix to this chapter).

We constructed an energy price index, WPI05NS, from the assumed energy prices and entered this index into the DRI Macro Model using appropriate Bureau of Labor Statistics weights. By constructing such an index we could obtain exogenous variables (production, labor compensation, and productivity indexes; capacity utilization measures; and investment and consumption indicators) that are consistent with the energy prices in each of the four scenarios. The price index is defined as:

$$WPI05NS = 0.071 * COAL + 0.097 * NATGAS + 0.254 * ELECT \\ + 0.86 * CRUDE + 0.283 * GAS + 0.141 * DIST \\ + 0.02 * RESID + 0.048 * OTHERREFINEDPDTS$$

where *COAL* = price index of coal, *NATGAS* = price index of natural gas, *ELECT* = price index of electricity, *CRUDE* = price index of crude petroleum, *GAS* = price index of gasoline, *DIST* = price index of distillate fuels, *RESID* = price index of residual fuels, and *OTHER-REFINEDPDTS* = price index of all other petroleum products (proxied by *DIST*).

In addition, the price and quantity of imported crude oil are adjusted so that the price of imports equals domestic oil price in each of the two alternatives and quantity of imports reflects U.S. import elasticity at the given price of crude oil. This elasticity is obtained from DRI Macro Model simulations OPEC ZERO 7/1 and OPEC TWO 7/1 (see the appendix for calculations). The model is run for both $7 and $11 assumptions about the price of crude oil; thus eight sets of exogenous variables are developed (one for each of the four scenarios assuming $7 crude oil and one for each assuming $11 crude). The adjusted price model is run by retrieving each of these sets of exogenous variables so direct and indirect influences of energy prices at all stages of processing can be considered.

Data

Although the energy prices themselves are discussed elsewhere, a description of the energy price indexes used in this model is in order.

Under the $11-per-barrel crude oil assumption, the energy price index rises steadily to 2.212 in 1980, then declines at 0.5 percent per year to the end of the forecast interval in the business as usual (BAU) scenario. In the business as usual with conservation (BAUWC) scenario, the energy price index rises to a level of 2.131 in 1980, then declines at about 0.4 percent per year. In the accelerated development (AD) scenario, this price index rises to a peak of 2.177 in 1977, then declines at a rate of 1.1 percent per year. Finally, in the combined conservation and accelerated development (CCAD) scenario, the energy price index (WPI05NS) rises only slightly to 2.088 in 1980, then declines by about 1.5 percent per year. Intermediate processed fuels and lubricants (WPISOP2400) falls from 1975 to 1977, then peaks in 1980 and declines again in all four scenarios.

Under the $7 crude oil assumption, the BAU scenario has WPI05NS declining sharply to a 1977 level of 1.666, then rising slowly. In the BAUWC scenario the index declines more, to a 1977 low of 1.586, then rises until 1980, after which it is virtually constant. In the AD scenario, WPI05NS declines to 1.556 in 1977, and rises by about 2.5 percent per year to 1980, after which it rises by about 0.3 percent per year. In the CCAD scenario, the index falls sharply to 1.586, then rises by 0.2 percent per year to 1980, then is constant at 1.594. In the BAU scenario, WPISOP2400 has a 1977 trough and 1980 peak similar to that just described, but in the other three scenarios it declines until 1977; then it rises continually throughout the period—rapidly through 1980 and by small increments thereafter.

Generally, the $11 assumption provides a WPI05NS that rises to 1980, and then declines while in the $7 assumption the price index declines at first, then rises after 1977. The difference between scenarios is therefore not a difference in direction of energy price movements, since they all rise and fall at the same time, but a difference in the magnitudes of these movements (see Figures 8-1, 8-2, and 8-3).

Results

It is difficult to briefly summarize the behavior of more than eighty prices that are forecast by the stages of processing model. In an effort to do so,

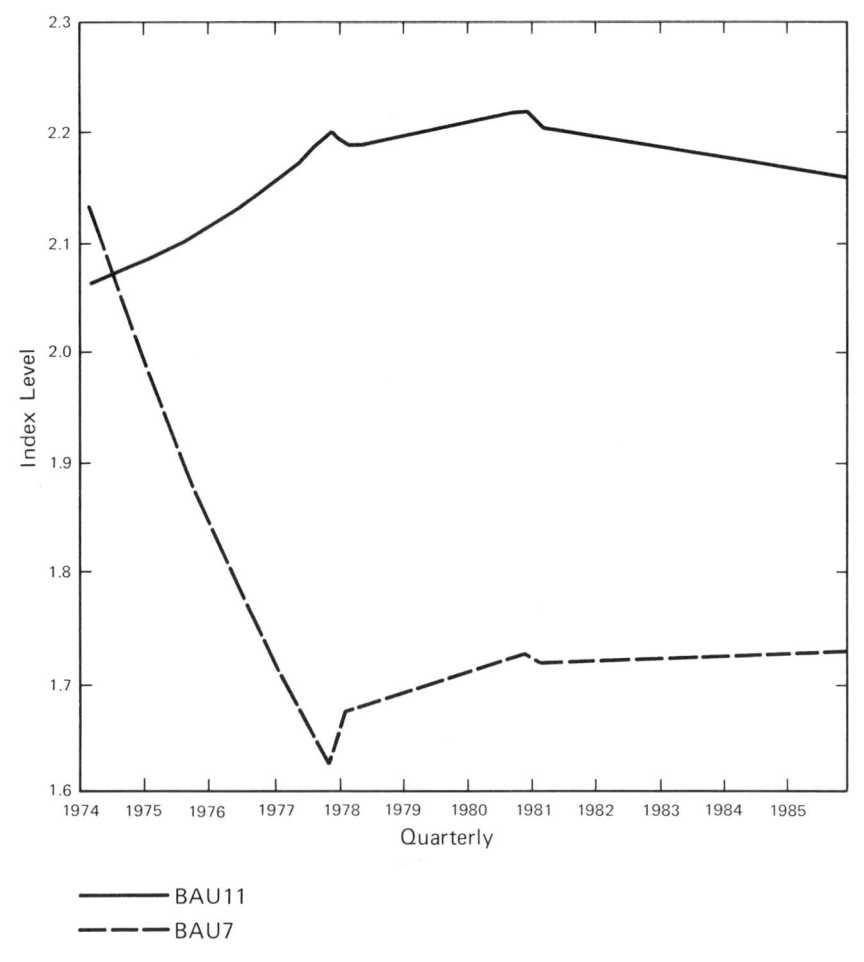

Figure 8-1. BAU11 versus BAU7 Energy Indexes.

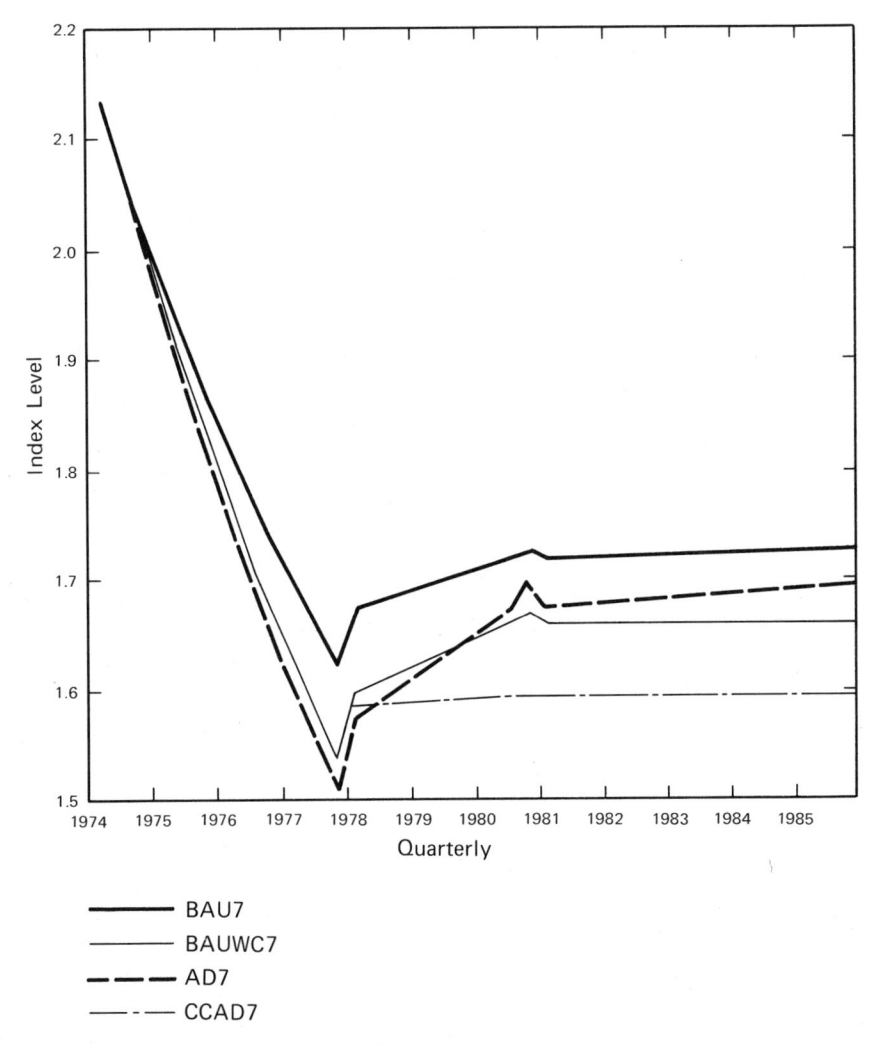

Figure 8-2. $7 Scenarios.

we concentrate on four- and six-digit WPIs and virtually ignore the eight-digit Wholesale Price Indexes. By doing this we hope to provide a reasonable balance between disaggregation and clarity. In the following discussion, a price index is called "lower" if its value is less than that in the business as usual case for the period in question. This term does not mean the index has fallen over time.

While most results are consistent with expectations, some results from the model deviate from expectations. Because of generally lower energy prices in alternative solutions, other aggregate prices are lower than in the business as usual case. As a result of this reduction in inflation,

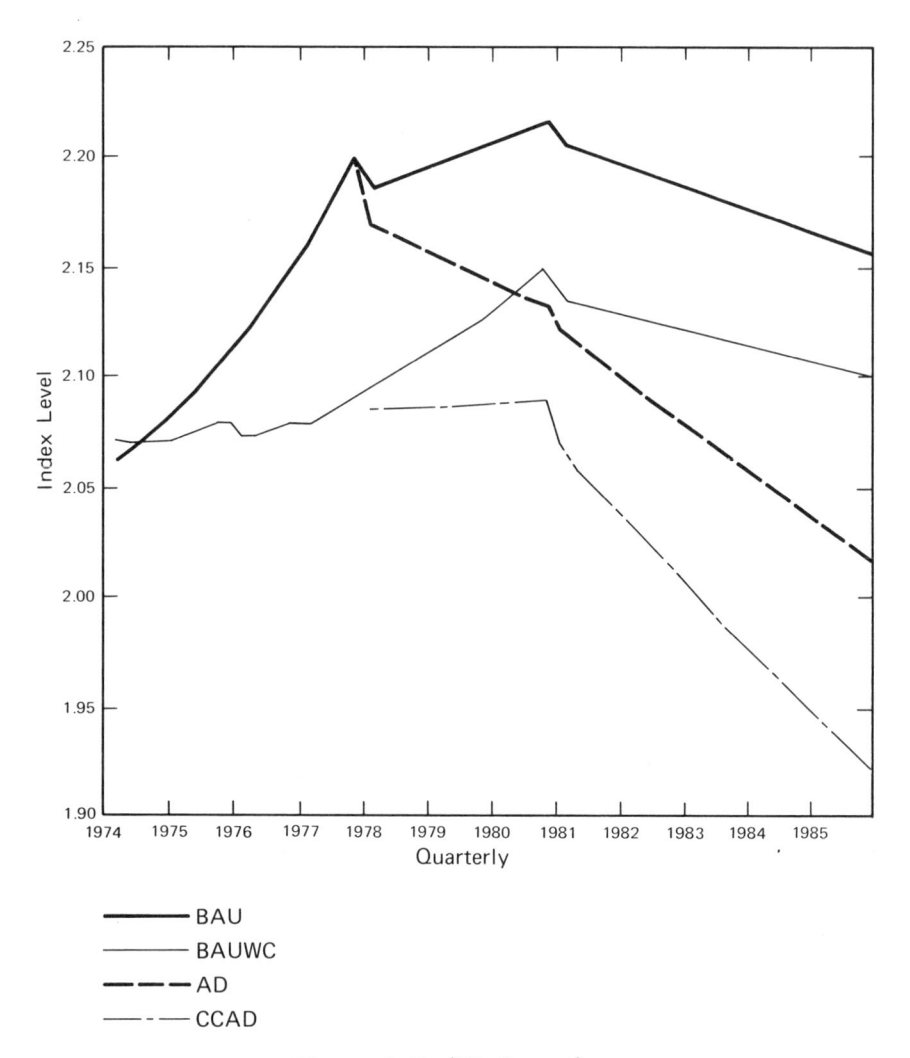

Figure 8–3. $11 Scenarios.

most indicators of economic activity—including capacity utilization, investment, and output—are higher. Surprises are not provided by these aggregate measures but rather by the movement of prices at relatively disaggregate levels and by the magnitudes of these movements.

The three strategies to reduce excess demand for energy have the effect of reducing the prices forecast in this model when compared to their values in the base case (BAU).

Viewed in a stages of processing context, materials for durable manufacturing and construction materials and components are most responsive to the price of energy while producer durables and consumer nondurables are not so responsive. This difference in impact is the result of the more direct influence of energy prices on intermediate stages of processing (materials and components) than on final stages (producer and consumer goods).

As Tables 8–1 and 8–2 indicate, alternative energy prices have the greatest influence on the prices of chemicals, iron and steel, nonferrous metals, and nonmetallic mineral products (WPI06, WPI101, WPI102, and WPI103), which are the most energy-intensive sectors of the model.

The prices of electrical machinery and equipment, rubber and plastic products, and industrial equipment of various types (WPI117, WPI07, WPI114, and WPI116) are relatively unaffected.

Each of these sectors is somewhat less energy-intensive than others in the model except for rubber and plastics, which uses large amounts of petroleum. The petroleum cost reduction in rubber and plastics is substantially counterbalanced by increased economic activity. In rough terms, a rightward shift in the marginal cost curve is coupled with a rightward shift in demand for rubber and plastics at any given moment under the alternative price schemes.

Under the $7 crude oil assumption, as a result of the turning points in energy prices, 1977 shows the largest differences from the base case in the conservation and the combined alternatives. Accelerated development produces its greatest price differences in 1980. These are generalizations, since lags of as much as one year are present under all scenarios. Under the $11 crude assumption, 1977–1978 generally shows the greatest price differences in the accelerated development case, while the conservation and combined alternatives show the difference to be greatest in 1980–1981. These energy price turning points, kinks in the price indexes (see Figures 8–2 and 8–3), result in the largest differences between alternatives and the base case. Generally, these kinks occur in 1977 or 1980.

There was a steady decline in the level of price indexes for plastic construction products (WPI0721) and structural clay products (WPI1340) under all scenarios and both crude oil price assumptions, because the cost of a major input (energy) is declining over time.

Conclusions

If the policy choice were based solely on a reduction in inflation, the combined strategy (i.e., conservation and accelerated development) presents itself as a better choice than conservation alone; more prices are reduced in more periods regardless of whether crude is based at $7 or $11. Using this criterion for policy selection, the results suggest that if crude

Table 8-1
Peak Difference Between Business as Usual and Combined Conservation and Accelerated Development ($7)

0% ≤ Diff < 2.0%	2.0% ≤ Diff < 2.5%	2.5% ≤ Diff < 3.0%	3.0% ≤ Diff < 3.5%	3.5% ≤ Diff
Tires (WPI071201)	Fasteners (WPI1081)	Steel mill products (WPI1013)	Paint (WPI0621)	Industrial chemicals (WPI0610)
Rubber belts (WPI071301)	Lighting fixtures (WPI1083)	Primary nonferrous shapes (WPI1022)	Foundry shop products (WPI1015)	Paint materials (WPI0622)
Plastic construction products (WPI0721)	Pumps and compressors (WPI1141)	Fabricated metal products (WPI1107)	Nonferrous metal (WPI102)	Insulation board (WPI0921)
Wire and cable (WPI1026)	Material handling (WPI1144)	Metal tanks (WPI1072)	Nonferrous scrap (WPI1023)	Iron and steel (WPI101)
Hardware (WPI1040)	Valves and fittings (WPI114901)	Miscellaneous metal products (WPI1108)	Sheet metal products (WPI1073)	Alloy basic shapes (WPI1024)
Plumbing fixtures (WPI1050)	Wiring devices (WPI1171)	Other miscellaneous products (WPI1089)	Structural metal products (WPI1073)	Mill shapes (WPI1025)
Heating equipment (WPI1060)	Transformers (WPI1174)		Construction machinery and equipment (WPI1120)	Fans and blowers (WPI1147)
Metal doors (WPI1071)	Storage batteries (WPI117901)		Ball and roller bearings (WPI114905)	Structural clay products (WPI1340)
Metalworking machinery and equipment (WPI1130)	Internal combustion engines (WPI1194)			Refractories (WPI1350)
Abrasive products (WPI1136)				
General purpose machinery and equipment (WPI1140)				Insulation materials (WPI1392)
Fluid power equipment (WPI1143)				
Mechanical power transmission equipment (WPI1145)				
Special industrial machinery and equipment (WPI1160)				

Electrical machinery
and equipment
(WPI1170)
Instruments (WPI1172)
Motors and generators
(WPI1173)
Switchgear (WPI1175)
Electronic components
(WPI1178)
Concrete products
(WPI1330)

Note: Diff $= \left[\dfrac{\text{Price}_{\text{BAU}} - \text{Price}_{\text{CCAD}}}{\text{Price}_{\text{BAU}}} \right] * 100$

Table 8–2
Peak Difference Between Business as Usual and Combined Conservation and Accelerated Development ($11)

$0\% \leq Diff < 2.0\%$	$2.0\% \leq Diff < 2.5\%$	$2.5\% \leq Diff < 3.0\%$	$3.0\% \leq Diff < 3.5\%$	$3.5\% \leq Diff$
Tires (WPI071201)[a]	Insulation board (WPI0921)[a]	Paint (WPI0621)	Nonferrous metals (WPI102)	Industrial chemicals (WPI0610)
Rubber belts (WPI071303)[a]	Primary nonferrous shapes (WPI1022)	Steel mill products (WPI1013)	Mill shapes (WPI1025)	Paint materials (WPI0622)
Plastic construction products (WPI0721)	Wire and cable (WPI1026)	Metal tanks (WPI1072)	Fabricated metal products (WPI107)	Iron and steel (WPI101)
Hardware (WPI1040)	Miscellaneous metal products (WPI1108)	Other miscellaneous metal products (WPI1089)	Construction machinery and equipment (WPI1120)	Foundry shop products (WPI1015)
Plumbing fixtures (WPI1050)	Fasteners (WPI1081)		Fans and blowers (WPI1147)	Nonferrous scrap (WPI1023)
Heating equipment (WPI1060)	Pumps and compressors (WPI1141)		Ball and roller bearings (WPI114905)	Alloy basic shapes (WPI1024)
Metal doors (WPI1071)	Storage batteries (WPI117901)			Sheet metal products (WPI1073)
Lighting fixtures (WPI1083)	Internal combustion engines (WPI1194)			Structural metal products (WPI1074)
Metalworking machinery and equipment (WPI1130)				Structural clay products (WPI1340)
Abrasive products (WPI1136)				Refractories (WPI1350)
General purpose machinery and equipment (WPI1140)				Insulation materials (WPI1392)
Fluid power equipment (WPI1143)				
Material handling equipment (WPI1144)				

Mechanical power transmission equipment (WPI1145)
Valves and fittings (WPI114901)
Special industrial machinery and equipment (WPI1160)
Electrical machinery and equipment (WPI1170)
Wiring devices (WPI1171)
Instruments (WPI1172)
Motors and generators (WPI1173)[a]
Transformers (WPI1174)
Switchgear (WPI1175)
Electronic components (WPI1178)
Concrete products (WPI1330)[a]

Note: Diff = $\left[\dfrac{\text{Price}_{\text{BAU}} - \text{Price}_{\text{CCAD}}}{\text{Price}_{\text{BAU}}} \right] * 100$

[a] Price index is higher by the specified percentage rather than lower.

oil is priced at $7, the combined strategy is best and conservation is second best. If crude oil is priced at $11, accelerated development is least effective at holding down inflation and the combined strategy may be marginally more effective than conservation. The reason many product prices are higher as a result of lower energy prices is the stimulated economic activity that results from these lowered prices. Increases in investment and production have offset energy cost decreases in influencing these prices (i.e., market influences outweigh cost influences in some years for some prices). Generally, prices that are higher in the alternatives are the less volatile ones.

For 1975 to 1978, conservation dampens inflation more than accelerated development in all stages dealt with by the model. In 1979 and thereafter, accelerated development is generally a more effective solution than conservation. In all cases, combined conservation and accelerated development is the most effective solution for reducing the energy components of inflation.

Appendix 8A

Fuels and related products, and power:

$WPI05NS = 0.071*COAL + 0.097*NATGAS$
$\qquad + 0.254*ELECT + 0.086*CRUDE + 0.283*GAS$
$\qquad + 0.141*DIST + 0.020*RESID + 0.048*OTHER$

Intermediate fuel:

$WPISOP2400 = (1.808*ELECT + 0.168*NATGAS$
$\qquad + 0.404*DIST + 0.525*GAS + 0.140*RESID$
$\qquad + 0.089*OTHER)/3.13$

Final Fuel:

$WPIFUELFMN = (0.062*COAL + 1.414*GAS$
$\qquad + 0.591*DIST + 0.197*OTHER)/2.26$

Import elasticity for oil:

$$= \frac{\%\Delta \text{import of crude oil (\$67) with \$2 change in petroleum price}}{\%\Delta \text{unit value of crude oil (\$67) with \$2 change in petroleum price}}$$

75:4	76:1	76:2	76:3	76:4 to 85:4
−0.125	−0.135	−0.177	−0.263	−0.266

About the Contributors

Christopher Alt is a systems analyst with the Federal Energy Administration. After obtaining the B.A. from Bowdoin College, he received the M.B.A. in information systems analysis from the Wharton Graduate School of Finance and Economics at the University of Pennsylvania. He is a coauthor of the *National Petroleum Product Supply and Demand* series of publications.

Scott E. Atkinson is chief of the Fuel Substitution Studies Branch, Federal Energy Administration. Dr. Atkinson received the B.A. from Williams College, the M.A. in economics from the University of Northern Colorado, and the Ph.D. in economics from the University of Colorado.

Anthony Bopp was chief of the Petroleum Modeling Branch at the Federal Energy Administration and is an assistant professor at Madison College, Harrisonburg, Virginia. He obtained the B.A. in English and the M.A. and Ph.D. in economics from the University of Missouri–Columbia. He is a coauthor of *National Petroleum Product Supply and Demand* series of publications.

Derriel Cato is an economist with the Federal Energy Administration. He received the B.A. from the University of South Carolina and is a candidate for the Ph.D. in economics at the University of Florida.

Paul H. Earl is an economist with Data Resources, Inc., and an assistant professor of economics at Georgetown University. Dr. Earl received the B.A. from Bucknell University and the M.A. and Ph.D. in economics from Georgetown University.

Robert Halvorsen is assistant professor of economics at the University of Washington–Seattle. Dr. Halvorsen received the B.A. from the University of Michigan and the M.B.A. and Ph.D. (economics) from Harvard University.

Arthur Kraft is professor of economics and management science at the University of Nebraska–Lincoln. He has served as a Federal Faculty Fellow at the Social Security Administration, and has taught at Ohio University. He received the Ph.D. in economics from the State University of New York at Buffalo.

George Lady is an economist with the Federal Energy Administration and the director of the Office of Coal, Nuclear and Electric Power Analysis.

He obtained the A.B. and A.M. in economics from the George Washington University and the Ph.D. from Johns Hopkins University.

Steven G. Phillips is an economist with Data Resources, Inc. He received the B.A., M.A., and Ph.D. in economics from Georgetown University.

Eugene Reiser is a mathematician in the Division of International Energy Analysis in the Federal Energy Administration. He received the B.S. in engineering from Akron University and the Ph.D. in mathematics from the University of Pittsburgh.

Mark Rodekohr is chief of the Natural Gas Modeling Branch, Federal Energy Administration. He received the B.S. from the University of Delaware and the M.A. and Ph.D. (economics) from the University of Colorado.

James Sweeney is an associate professor of engineering/economic systems at Stanford University, and was previously director of the Office of Energy Systems, Federal Energy Administration. Dr. Sweeney received the B.S. from M.I.T. and the M.A. and Ph.D. from Stanford University in engineering/economic systems.

Noel D. Uri is an economist in the Division of Electric Power Analysis, Federal Energy Administration. The author of *Towards an Efficient Allocation of Electrical Energy,* Dr. Uri received the A.B. in mathematics from San Diego State University and the Ph.D. in economics from the University of Illinois.

About the Editors

A. Bradley Askin heads the National Impact Division in the Federal Energy Administration. He originally joined FEA as a Federal Faculty Fellow on academic leave from the Graduate School of Administration, University of California–Irvine. While on the faculty at Irvine, Dr. Askin served as a consultant to the Price Commission and was associated with the Rand Corporation. He received the Ph.D. in economics from the Massachusetts Institute of Technology.

John Kraft is director of the Office of Macroeconomic Impact Analysis, Federal Energy Administration. Prior to holding his current position, he headed the Division of Econometric Modeling and Research at FEA. He has also taught at the University of Florida, and he served as a Brookings Institution Economic Policy Fellow. He received the Ph.D. in economics from the University of Pittsburgh.